Why Work?

Christian College Coalition Study Guides
Edited by John A. Bernbaum

Why Work?

Careers and Employment in Biblical Perspective

John A. Bernbaum
and Simon M. Steer

Baker Book House
Grand Rapids, Michigan 49506

Christian College Coalition
Washington, D.C. 20036

Excerpts from the Encyclical "On Human Work," John Paul II, September 14, 1981, published by the United States Catholic Conference, Washington, D.C., are used with permission. Excerpts from Paul Marshall, "Vocation, Work, and Jobs," and from Edward Vanderkloet, "Why Work Anyway?" from *Labour of Love: Essays on Work*, published by Wedge Publishing Foundation, are used with permission. Excerpts from Martin E. Clark, *Choosing Your Career: The Christian's Decision Manual*, published by Presbyterian and Reformed Publishing Company, are used with permission.

Unless otherwise noted, Scripture references are from the Holy Bible: New International Version. Copyright © 1973, 1978, 1984 International Bible Society. Used by permission of Zondervan Bible Publishers. Other translations used are the King James Version (KJV), the New American Standard Bible (NASB), and the Revised Standard Version (RSV).

ISBN: 0–8010–0933–2

Printed in the United States of America

The Christian College Coalition, an association of more than seventy colleges, was founded in 1976. With main offices located in Washington, D.C., the coalition serves a vital sector of American private higher education—regionally accredited liberal arts colleges committed both to being excellent educational institutions and to keeping the Christian faith central to every facet of campus life. All member colleges seek faculty and administrators who are academically qualified, personally committed to the Christian faith, and determined to integrate that faith into their academic disciplines and daily lives.

The coalition brings member colleges into a cooperative relationship that strengthens them by enabling them to achieve common goals. It has steadily grown in membership and expanded the breadth of activities it offers to member colleges. These schools, affiliated with nearly thirty denominations, find enrichment in the diversity of religious traditions within the coalition, a diversity that draws upon a core of common concern for biblical values and truths. For further information write to:

Christian College Coalition
1776 Massachusetts Avenue, N.W.
Washington, DC 20036

Contents

Introduction

Meet someone for the first time and it is a safe bet that within the first five minutes you will have asked the question "What do you do?" The frequent occurrence of the question indicates more than a lack of originality in our small talk. It also points to the idolization of jobs and careers in modern Western culture. Occupation has become a primary criterion for assessing personal worth—we are what we do.

Consider the sacrifices we lay at the feet of this modern-day idol: the sacrifice of money spent on college tuition fees; of time (measured in years) given over to medical school, law school, or other forms of training; of energy expended in study and preparation, often at hours when most civilized people are quite unconscious!

Such dedication to academic pursuits and vocational training is usually seen as commendable and worthwhile. It is possible, however, for commitment to study and career to become a modern form of idolatry. It is particularly sad when Christians are among those bowing the knee. Unfortunately Christians frequently adopt the same values and objectives as non-Christians with regard to jobs and careers. On both Christian and secular college campuses, the questions most frequently asked are, "What is the job market going to be like when I graduate?" "What courses do I need to make myself more attractive to potential employers?" "What skills do I need in order to get a good job?" Are these really the questions that Christians should be asking?

Similarly, a typical conversation among recent college graduates (embryonic Yuppies, if you like), might go something like this: "I want to find a job in which I can be happy." "I want to find a job that is fulfilling." "I want to be a vice president by the time I'm thirty-five." "I should be at thirty thousand dollars in five years' time." These are comments that result from a secular rather than a Christian view of work.

In order to arrive at a Christian understanding of work, we must first answer the foundational question: "Why work?" Various cultures and philosophies provide different answers. At the heart of the rhetoric of Marxism is the cry "Workers of the world unite," and the continuing appeal of communism is at least partly based upon its deification of work and the workers. By means of work, poverty can be alleviated, injustice corrected, the socialist personality perfected, and the glory of the state promoted. The reality of the situation, however, is quite the opposite. Workers in Marxist states continue to be an oppressed class who are tightly controlled by Communist Party elites. Work and workers are deified in Marxist rhetoric but exploited for the advantage of the state and its ruling class.

In the economic system and philosophy we know as capitalism, the answer to the question "Why work?" can be traced back to Adam Smith's classic treatise *The Wealth of Nations*. The key here is the pursuit of enlightened self-interest which in turn contributes to the "common good." Capitalism in this sense is a harnessing of the innate selfishness of humanity for the benefit of all. We are quick to praise the productivity and creativity that this philosophy can foster, but we must also remember that in contemporary American society, it has frequently led to an addiction to self-interest and material gain.

A third answer is provided by a false version of American Christianity, best described as Christian dualism. The sacred and the secular are viewed as separate realms which should remain independent of one another. God and mammon can both be served in the "American way of life," as long as we refrain from mixing religion with economics and business. In this approach, attitudes toward jobs and careers stem more from capitalist principles than from biblical precepts.

In the face of these distortions, the biblical answer to the question "Why work?" is remarkably comprehensive and penetrating. There are fifteen Hebrew words which are translated "work" in the King James Version of the Bible and one of those words is used more than 150 times! The Greek word *ergon*, meaning "work," is also used frequently in the New Testament.

As we study Scripture's teaching on this subject, the following principles emerge. First, work is a God-ordained function. It is part of God's original intention for humanity and not a result of the fall. The earliest job description occurs in the creation account in which God commands humanity to "fill the earth and subdue it; and have dominion" (Gen. 1:28, RSV). This job description comes from One who himself is a worker. The psalmist describes God in the following terms: "Thou hast made the moon to mark the seasons. . . . Thou makest darkness. . . . O LORD, how manifold are thy works!" (Ps. 104:19, 20, 24, RSV). It is of considerable significance that in the middle of this description of the working, creating God, there is a reference to human labor. Verse 23 of this psalm reads, "Man goes forth to his work and to his labor until the evening" (RSV). The clear suggestion is that human labor must be conducted as part of the divine creative enterprise. It is striking that no other religion holds to a belief in a God who works. The teaching surrounding the fourth commandment (concerning the Sabbath day) also implies that work is an integral part of God's divine purpose.

Second, as a result of the fall, work is no longer the pure joy that God intended it to be. The blessing became a burden and the joy became toil. This profound change is described in Genesis 3:16–19, a passage which emphasizes that the labor of childbirth will be fraught with pain, as will other types of physical labor. The biblical account of the fall, then, points to two of the most common abuses of work. First, it can become a means of exploitation and oppression, a condition described in James 5:4, where the writer accuses the rich of exploiting the poor laborers. Second, work can become an idol. Scripture often defines such idolatry as an excessive concern for acquiring material possessions. The vanity of accumulating wealth (see Eccles. 2:4–11; 5:10) is a manifestation of idolizing work. In our own day this aspect of idolatry is coupled with the assessment of a person's social status on the basis of that person's job. This in turn cultivates attitudes of pride, envy, and insecurity.

The third major biblical principle is that work has been redeemed from the curse by Jesus Christ. Through the redemption brought about by the death of Christ, work as blessing prevails over work as curse. The fact that the eternal Son of God worked at a carpenter's bench is an extraordinary testimony to the sanctity of common work. The apostle Paul, too, set an example of honest labor by working as a tentmaker.

The fourth principle is that work is to be done as a service to Christ. This was to be the attitude even of first-century slaves, for Paul writes: "Slaves, obey in everything those who are your earthly masters, not with eyeservice, as men-pleasers, but in singleness of heart, fearing the Lord. Whatever your task, work heartily, as serving the Lord and not men, knowing that from the Lord you will receive the inheritance as your reward; you are serving the Lord Christ" (Col. 3:22–24, rsv). Work is to be part of our sacred stewardship as believers and in this vital sense all our jobs come within the realm of the sacred. This is beautifully illustrated in Exodus 31, in which the work of craftsmen and laborers in the construction of "the tent of meeting" is the result of God's gift of his Spirit. Similarly, the New Testament concept of the priesthood of all believers implies that all our work is a spiritual service.

Finally, the Bible tells us that work not only brings glory to God if done for him, but has moral benefits as well. In 2 Thessalonians 3:10–12, Paul instructs us that we should work in order to provide for ourselves and our families. Those who can work but choose not to are severely reprimanded—if they will not work, they do not deserve to eat.

We also work in order to share the benefits with those who are in need, and so our good works will be a witness for Christ before others, thereby bringing glory to his name.

If we are to transform the prevailing idolatrous approach to the subject of jobs and careers into a thoroughly biblical view, we will need to convert the biblical principles we have discussed into attitudes of mind and heart. We will need to begin viewing our work with a new sense of vigor and dignity, recognizing that these are God-ordained activities. Work is part of our stewardship; it enables us to provide for ourselves, our families, and those in need. Unless our job involves us in activities clearly contrary to the will of God, it is a sacred task inasmuch as we do it as unto the Lord. In this sense, we are all in full-time Christian service, and this should motivate us to produce work of the highest quality.

We will also need to rid ourselves of job-market myths that secular thinking has created. The notion that a job should bring fulfillment is a dangerous half-truth, in that the Bible never indicates that our jobs should be "fun" or make us "happy." Fulfillment is more correctly understood in the sense of service, taking pleasure in the contribution that our work is making to the community. This implies that whenever possible we should choose work that benefits those in need and this should head the list of criteria by which a Christian chooses a career.

It is an illusion to seek fulfillment in our jobs. If we view decisions about our careers through the lens of self-satisfaction or self-interest, we are not being biblical people. We must replace our lens. Disciples of Jesus Christ must view career decisions not through the lens of self-fulfillment but through the lens of the needs of God's people—indeed, of human needs whenever they are found. That is God's intention for us.

In God's wisdom, when we willingly give up our own desires for self-advancement in order to serve others who are less fortunate, he graciously gives in return a sense of peace and joy unmatched by any worldly reward or recognition, because we are doing what he made us to do. We are being truly human.

This study guide is dedicated to helping Christians rediscover a biblical vision for why we work. Far too many recent Christian publications have merely baptized the Yuppie mentality of our North American culture. Disciples of Jesus Christ must be prepared to challenge these cultural influences that are distorting the gospel message.

The Bible offers a radically different answer to the question "Why work?"—if we are willing to listen and then respond accordingly. For the Christian, work is not a four-letter word—not an idol nor a curse. By working, human beings continue to fulfill God's command to subdue the earth. We are instructed by God to make the most of his creation and to assist in a more extensive distribution of the good things of that creation. So let us, as disciples of Jesus Christ, be supernatural workers, whatever our task, working heartily as serving the Lord.

1
Biblical Starting Points

The First Job Description

The first job description consisted of six words: "Fill the earth and subdue it" (Gen. 1:28). A little vague perhaps, a little open-ended, suitable only for overachievers, but a job description nonetheless. At the outset of human experience there was an instruction to work. God called Adam and Eve to control, arrange, and develop the world that God has created. They were to be co-creators with him. God intended this to be a joyous and fulfilling task carried out in perfect harmony with himself. The starting point of any discussion of a Christian view of work is the recognition that labor is a God-ordained activity, part of God's original purpose for the human race.

In this first section, we will examine this foundational theological principle by juxtaposing two analyses of the subject; the first by Carl F. H. Henry in *Aspects of Christian Social Ethics* and the second an extract from Pope John Paul II's 1981 encyclical *On Human Work*. Henry writes:

> Through his work, man shares the creation-purpose of God in subduing nature, whether he be a miner with dirty hands, a mechanic with greasy face, or a stenographer with stencil-smudged

fingers. Work is permeated by purpose; it is intended to serve God, benefit mankind, make nature subservient to the moral program of creation. Man must therefore apply his whole being—heart and mind, as well as hand—to the daily job. As God's fellow-worker he is to reflect God's creative activity on Monday in the factory no less than on Sunday when commemorating the day of rest and worship.

To consider work a channel of divine creation, by which the creature serves God and man, carries certain consequences for one's attitude toward labor. The Christian becomes morally obligated to withhold producing, and even purchasing (since money is the conversion of his talent into cash) culturally worthless, let alone wicked and harmful, items. Nor will he engage in their promotion or distribution. As Treglown remarks, "There can be no sense of purpose in making trash." In this regard, the Church has sensed too little its potentially constructive impact on industry; it has not fully sensitized the conscience of the Christian worker to God's purpose for human labor on the basis of creation (p. 48).

The relevance of Christian teaching is demonstrated in Henry's statement that "work is permeated by purpose." For many in our society, work has become purposeless, a merely mechanical process that is indicated by the expression *make a living*. For others, work certainly has a compelling purpose, but it is a distorted one, namely, the accumulation of wealth and the enhancement of social status. In contrast, Henry stresses that the purpose of work is to "serve God, benefit mankind, [and] make nature subservient to the moral program of creation."

Henry also touches on a much-neglected implication of the fact that we are co-creators with God. Two provocative sentences demand discussion: "The Christian becomes morally obligated to withhold producing, and even purchasing . . . culturally worthless, let alone wicked and harmful, items. Nor will he engage in their promotion or distribution." Theology is thus a vital component of something as practical as the selection of a job. It is to be regretted that most of the popular Christian literature on the subject of vocational guidance neglects cultural worth as a criterion for choosing a career. Of course, Christians will sometimes disagree on what is culturally worthless, but we should all determine to analyze vocational alternatives on the basis of what Henry calls "the moral program of creation."

Let us now consider an extract from the 1981 papal encyclical:

Man has to subdue the earth and dominate it, because as the "image of God" he is a person, that is to say, a subjective being capable of acting in a planned and rational way, capable of deciding about himself and with a tendency to self-realization. As a person, man is therefore the subject of work. As a person he works, he performs various actions belonging to the work process; independently of their objective content, these actions must all serve to realize his humanity, to fulfill the calling to be a person that is his by reason of his very humanity.

And so this "dominion" spoken of in the biblical text . . . refers not only to the objective dimension of work, but at the same time introduces us to an understanding of its subjective dimension. Understood as a process whereby man and the human race subdue the earth, work corresponds to this basic biblical concept only when throughout the process man manifests himself and confirms himself as the one who "dominates." This dominion, in a certain sense, refers to the subjective dimension even more than to the objective one. This dimension conditions the very ethical nature of work. In fact there is no doubt that human work has an ethical value of its own, which clearly and directly remains linked to the fact that the one who carries it out is a person, a conscious and free subject, that is to say, a subject that decides about himself.

Such a concept practically does away with the very basis of the ancient differentiation of people into classes according to the kind of work done. This does not mean that from the objective point of view human work cannot and must not be rated and qualified in any way. It only means that the primary basis of the value of work is man himself, who is its subject. This leads immediately to a very important conclusion of an ethical nature: However true it may be that man is destined for work and called to it, in the first place work is "for man" and not man "for work" (pp. 13–14).

The characteristic Roman Catholic emphasis upon the dignity of every person as created in the image of God results in an understanding of the purpose of work that usefully complements that of Henry. According to the Roman Catholic view, the job description in Genesis contains a subjective as well as an objective element. Human beings are intended to realize their humanity through the fulfillment that comes from the task of "dominion."

8

We should notice that the traditional Roman Catholic distinction between sacred and secular that is so often criticized by Protestant theologians gives way in the papal encyclical to a repudiation of "the ancient differentiation of people into classes according to the kind of work done." The exaggerated attachment of status to certain occupations and the devaluation of others in our modern culture suggests that this comprehensive attitude of respect is deeply relevant.

Of Sweaty Brows and BMWs

The fall gets blamed for a lot of things. Christians have a tendency to excuse their dislikes by suggesting that had it not been for Adam and Eve's misbehavior in the Garden such things would never have been necessary. Work is one of the prime examples. We are eager to point out that one of the primary punishments for sin was that "by the sweat of your brow you will eat your food" (Gen 3:19)—paradise was lost and the nine-to-five day instituted. This, however, is a misuse of a theological principle and has often resulted in the exaggeration of the negative aspects of work at the expense of the positive.

As we have seen, our starting point must be a recognition of the divinely ordained nature of work. This places work in its essentially positive context. From there we can proceed to a realistic appraisal of the negative aspects of work that is carried out in a fallen world.

What are the fallen aspects of the nature of work? The first is the purpose of work. Human beings were intended to subdue the earth for God's glory but instead sought to exploit it for themselves. The second aspect is the mental and physical toil involved in work. Labor became tiring, frustrating, monotonous. The third aspect is the spoiling of working relationships. Conflict between labor and management, companies and clients, and disharmony in the workplace are examples of this. Whenever human beings are treated as mere tools of production, the objects rather than the subjects of work, the fallen nature of humanity is operative. A parallel of this is when unemployment is viewed as an unfortunate but largely unavoidable consequence of economic laws.

Modern American culture and particularly the so-called Yuppie generation reveals a more subtle element of the fallen nature of work, or more accurately, a fallen attitude toward work. This takes the form of idolizing upward mobility in one's career for the purpose of personal material gain and prestige. Rather than being a service to God and humanity, work is a source of purely personal fulfillment and a means to material prosperity. It is possible to view the Yuppie philosophy as a distorted attempt to redeem work from the toil and monotony so often associated with it by surrounding it with the glamorous trappings of a computerized consumer society. After all, isn't a BMW worth sweating for?

Christ and the Paradox of Work

The salvation that God offers us in Jesus Christ is intended to affect every part of our lives, including our work. As a result of Christ's death and resurrection we have been liberated from the grip of a fallen world. As new creatures in Christ, Christians are to have a Christ-centered orientation in life. This orientation has major implications for the way we work. The repentance that is part of faith in Christ involves a renunciation of the egotism that produces selfish motivations for working. Those who bemoan the necessity of work may repent of their resentment of the burdensome aspect of labor, learning to accept it as a consequence of living in a fallen world and even as a way of identifying with the suffering of Christ. Alternatively those who tend to idolize career and the status it brings, sometimes to the point of becoming workaholics, may experience the release of discovering that self-identity and personal worth come from knowing God rather than one's prospects for promotion or salary scale.

Our salvation is founded in One who himself worked at a carpenter's bench. He knew the toil of work, identifying himself with an aspect of the human condition that will persist until God's kingdom comes in its fullness. But Christ's identification with the worker gives our labor a dignity that can offset the drudgery. The sweaty brow remains a fact of life, but in Christ it becomes an element of servanthood.

Work and Works: The Difference an *s* Makes

A familiar distinction is made in theology between faith and works. The apostle Paul emphasized that personal salvation is a gift of God which we appropriate through faith in Christ. It can never be based on meritorious behavior or any claim of human righteousness (e.g., Eph. 2:8–9). It is perhaps unfortunate that attempts to earn salvation have so often been designated by the term *works*, for its negative connotation has carried over to Christian perspectives on work. The fact that Christians frown upon "works" as a basis for salvation has exacerbated the separation of sacred and secular whereby a person's work bears no relation to his Christian faith. It is of great importance, therefore, that we recognize the difference an *s* makes. The apostle Paul, and the early church generally, preached the value and imperative of work while rejecting works as a basis for salvation.

The letters of Paul contain many exhortations on work, including a sustained polemic against idleness (2 Thess. 3:6–12). Paul commended manual labor and himself worked as a tentmaker to support himself and others in need. When he encouraged slaves to work willingly as if they were slaves of Christ, he was not defending the institution of slavery but indicated the value of what in the eyes of society was the most menial work. His declaration that "if any one will not work, let him not eat" (2 Thess. 3:10, RSV) must not be taken as a lack of concern for those who cannot support themselves, but as an assertion that all Christians should be involved in useful activity. We need to recognize that our work is part of our worshipful service, carried out in gratitude to the One who has redeemed us.

To What Are We Called?

Christians are in the habit of saying such things as "I feel called to be a nurse" or "God has called me to be a minister." We speak of a "calling in life" and usually equate it with such terms as "career" and "vocation." In one way, this concern for calling reflects a commendable desire to be true to the will of God for one's life, but at the same time it is a potentially dangerous half-truth. By equating the biblical notion of calling with careers we run the risk of implying that every individual needs to discover the one occupation that has been divinely appointed for her. This leads to unnecessary anxiety in the choice of a career and a constant questioning of whether one is in the will of God.

It is therefore essential to gain a right understanding of what the New Testament writers mean when they use the term *calling*. This will be dealt with in more detail in chapter 3, but briefly we can say that calling is a remarkably rich concept referring to the entire process of salvation initiated by God in Christ. As Christians ours is a total calling to discipleship in the body of Christ (Rom. 1:7), to citizenship in the kingdom of God (1 Thess. 2:12), and to salvation (Rom. 11:29). The choice of a career therefore does not involve the search for a separate, distinct calling, but should be seen as an important part of our response to the all-encompassing call of God to salvation.

Study Questions

1. How would you write a fuller version of the first job description: "Fill the earth and subdue it" (Gen. 1:28)?
2. What do you think Carl Henry means when he says that work is intended to "make nature subservient to the moral program of creation"?
3. Does Henry's statement that "the Christian becomes morally obligated to withhold producing . . . culturally worthless items[,] nor will he engage in their promotion or distribution" suggest that jobs in advertising, marketing, and the manufacture of certain products are off limits to Christians?
4. What does the papal encyclical mean by the "subjective dimension" of work? If work is "for man" and not man "for work," what does this imply for the creation of new jobs in society?
5. Should Christians attempt to overcome the fallen aspects of work or merely accept them as a necessary evil?
6. According to Ephesians 2:8–10, what should be a Christian's motivation for working?

Biblical Passages for Further Study

Helpful insights about the following subjects can be gained by studying the biblical texts indicated:

1. Work as God's original purpose for men and women

   Genesis 1:26–28
   Psalm 8:3–4, 6

2. The "fallen nature" of work

   Genesis 3:19

3. Warnings against laziness

   Proverbs 6:6–11
   Proverbs 12:24, 27
   Proverbs 18:9
   Proverbs 24:30–34
   2 Thessalonians 3:6–8a

4. Admonitions to be diligent in our work

   2 Thessalonians 3:8b–10
   Ecclesiastes 9:10

5. Warnings about wealth becoming our idol

   Proverbs 11:28
   Ecclesiastes 5:10–17
   Luke 12:13–21
   1 Timothy 6:6–10, 17–19

6. Paul's instructions about our motives for working

   Colossians 3:22–24
   2 Thessalonians 3:10–12

2 Working Out Work: A Historical Survey

Hebrews 12:1 tells us that as Christians we are surrounded by "a great cloud of witnesses." In its original context this refers to the example provided by Old Testament heroes of the faith, men and women who inspire and challenge us by their obedience to the call of God. The premise of this chapter is that "the cloud of witnesses" also includes those who have taught, preached, and lived out the faith through centuries of church history. Human understanding of God's revelation is a dynamic process in which every generation of believers may learn from the insights and oversights of those who have gone before.

The church has understood the theology of work in different ways at different times. The record contains major blemishes (e.g., centuries of a false separation of sacred and secular), as well as periods of radical faithfulness to biblical truth (e.g., the Reformers' emphasis on all work as a service to God). In *Labour of Love*, Paul Marshall and Edward Vanderkloet provide a helpful survey of the major developments in the church's understanding of the nature, purpose, and conduct of work together with relevant comparisons with secular thinking. As we seek to apply biblical truth to the modern marketplace, let us be informed and guided by the great cloud of witnesses that unites past and present under Christ.

The Ancient World and Work[1]

When the biblical teaching is compared with the attitudes toward work of the educated in the Greek and Roman world, then it appears novel, startling, and quite electrifying. Most of the examples we have are from those who were more philosophically inclined; there isn't too much of a record from the ones who actually did most of the work.[2] Given this restriction, it is clear that the educated viewed what we now call work with some disdain, a disdain which extended toward those who were involved in such work.

One type of work which drew widespread condemnation was that of the artisan. Xenophon put the words in Socrates' mouth that "the illiberal arts (banausikai), as they are called, are spoken against, and are, naturally enough, held in utter disdain in our states . . . [they] leave no spare time for attention to one's friends and the city. . . . In fact, in some of the states, it is not even lawful for any of the citizens to work at illiberal arts."[3] Aristotle asked that citizens cultivate leisure, as "leisure is a necessity, both for growth in goodness and for the pursuit of political activities."[4] Isocrates held that citizenship rights should be restricted to those "who could afford the time and possessed sufficient means."[5] Later, Cicero used the term *sordidi* to describe the occupation of artisans, while the writers at the end of the Roman Republic had an ideal of *otium* (leisure) *cum dignitate*.[6]

At times there appeared to be something of a different view concerning those involved in agriculture. Xenophon thought that "even stouthearted warriors cannot live without the aid of work-

1. The rest of this chapter, except for the concluding study questions, consists of excerpts from Paul Marshall, "Vocation, Work, and Jobs," and Edward Vanderkloet, "Why Work Anyway?" both in *Labour of Love: Essays on Work* (Toronto: Wedge, 1980), pp. 1–19, 20–47.

2. On the attitude of those actually engaged in the work, see A. T. Geoghegan, *The Attitude Toward Labour in Early Christianity and Ancient Culture* (Washington, D.C.: Catholic University of America, 1945), pp. 48–54.

3. *Oeconomicus* 4.2, 3; Claud Mossé, *The Ancient World at Work* (London: Chatto and Windus, 1969), p. 25. See also Pierre Jacard, *Histoire sociale du travail* (Paris: Payot, 1960), pp. 66–75.

4. *Politics* 1329a.1–2.

5. *Areopagitica* 26.

6. *De officiis* 1.42, 150; Mossé, *The Ancient World at Work*, p. 25.

ers . . . those who stock and cultivate the land"; Aristotle thought that the "best kind of populace is one of farmers"; Cicero thought that "none is better than agriculture . . . none more becoming in a free man."[7]

The reason for this duality is contained in Cicero's qualifier *in a free man*. The idea of doing something with one's hands was not itself necessarily degrading. Even Homer's Odysseus could build his own boat and Penelope could spin and weave; Paris of Troy helped build his own house while Nausicäa did her brothers' laundry.[8] But this type of activity was freely chosen; it was independent. What was objected to was work and relations based on dependency and necessity—the absence of autonomy *(autarkeia)*. Freedom at the time of Aristotle consisted of "status, personal inviolability, freedom of economic activity and right of unrestricted movement."[9] The slaves, the majority of the population, lacked all of these, and the artisans, while under contract, lacked the last two for a limited time. Hence Aristotle thought that craftsmen were really part slaves, and therefore a bit less than fully human. In his list of "ways of life," he did not even bother to mention the craftsmen because it was obvious to him that such people were not free.[10]

This concern with absence of necessity carried over into attitudes toward farming. Aristotle ranked shepherds high because "the laziest are shepherds; for they get their food without labour *(ponos)* from tame animals and have leisure *(skholazousin)*."[11] Hesiod, the poet, praised farming, but he advised his brother,

7. *Oeconomicus* 4.15; *Politics* 1318b.1; *De officiis* 1.42. See also Alison Burford, *Craftsmen in Greek and Roman Society* (London: Thames and Hudson, 1972), especially pp. 29–30 on Cicero's attitude toward farmers; Geoghegan, *Attitude Toward Labour*, pp. 37–38.

8. Hannah Arendt, *The Human Condition* (New York: Doubleday, 1959), p. 290.

9. W. Westerman, "Between Slavery and Freedom," *American Historical Review* 50 (1945): 213–27. See also Edwin G. Kaiser, *Theology of Work* (Westminster, Md.: Newman, 1966), pp. 32ff.

10. *Nichomachaean Ethics* 1.5; *Eudaemonian Ethics* 1215a.35–36; *Politics* 1337b.5; Arendt, *The Human Condition*, p. 302; R. Schlaifer, "Greek Theories of Slavery from Homer to Aristotle," *Harvard Studies in Classical Philology* 47 (1936): 165–204.

11. *Politics* 1256a.30–31. Aristotle equated *skhole* and *aergia*, leisure and laziness. Cf. Arendt, *The Human Condition*, pp. 323–24.

"Make haste, you and your slaves alike . . . set your slaves to winnow Demeter's holy grain . . . put your bondman out of doors and look out for a servant girl with no children . . . let your men rest their poor knees."[12] No poor peasant this who must do his own work! Those who praised agriculture assumed that the actual farm labor was being done by slaves and servants. Their praise was for the landowner as the backbone of the political order.

A Comparison of Paul and Seneca

The only exceptions to this sort of view occurred in the stoic philosophers. Chryssipus reversed Aristotle's treatment of the servant in terms of the slave, and he considered slaves in the light of servants. He held that slaves were merely hired for life and that their rights were violated if they were actually possessed by the master. Stoic philosophy gave work a value of its own and held that it did not exclude one from a virtuous life.[13]

Despite this similarity, it is clear that many of the parallels between Christianity and stoicism have been badly overstated. We will try to show this by a brief comparison of Paul and Seneca. Seneca was a contemporary of Paul; indeed some scholars think they may even have met while Paul was in Rome. He was quite similar to Paul in some respects, and Calvin's first work was a commentary on his *De Clementia*.

However, Seneca tended to view the person as composed of two different things—body and soul—and the soul was definitely higher: "What else could you call such a soul than a God dwelling in a human body?" *(deus in corpore humano hospitans?)*. In this dualism the body was certainly essential; Seneca confessed to "an inborn affection for our body . . . we should cherish the body with great care." Nevertheless the body was "to be regarded as *necessary* rather than important." Seneca saw the soul residing in the body as beneath a heavy burden *(gravis sarcina)*; the body was a weight and a penance *(pondus ac poena)*, chains *(in vinculis)*,

---

12. *Works and Days* 1.383–617.

13. Ludwig Edelstein, *The Meaning of Stoicism* (Cambridge: Cambridge University Press, 1966), pp. 74–78.

and a prison *(carcer)*. In fact, he held that "to despise our bodies is pure freedom" *(contemptus corporis sui certa libertas est)*.[14]

In contrast to this, Paul emphasized that the resurrection was the resurrection of the *body*. He held that the body was not a prison, but the *temple* of the Holy Spirit; in fact he usually used the expression *your bodies* in such a way that it meant "yourselves." For Paul "spirit" *(pneuma)* was never a distinct *part* of man, and the best translation of *psyche* in his writings is probably "life." The war between "flesh" and "spirit" was a war not between body and soul, but between tendencies to obedience and disobedience.[15]

These two different views of mankind gave rise to two different views of work. Seneca certainly thought that nobility of mind could be found in all classes, for "Socrates was no aristocrat. Cleanthes worked at a well and served as a hired man watering a garden. Philosophy did not find Plato a nobleman; it made him one." Everyone could enter the "households . . . of noblest intellects." But, in his scheme, this only meant that such work was not a barrier to the higher life. Philosophical activity was still the best sort of life; Seneca was only saying that all sorts of people could enter now into it. In fact, he thought that the "common sort" of arts were "concerned with equipping life; there is in them no pretence to beauty or honour."[16] Such a view was in marked contrast to Paul, who viewed all types of work, mental or physical, as potentially equal service to the Lord.

Pre-Reformation Christianity

We have compared the New Testament with other ancient views rather extensively in order to doubly emphasize the Bible's distinctiveness. Even compared to the stoic philosophers, who were the most generous in their appraisal of necessary work, the biblical authors stand out starkly in their praise of even the

14. J. N. Sevenster, *Paul and Seneca* (Leiden: E. J. Brill, 1961), pp. 69, 72; *Epistolae* 14.1, 2; 23.6; 24.17; 31.11; 62.22; 76.25; 79.12; 92.33; *De consolatione ad Helvian* 11.6.

15. 1 Cor. 6:15, 19–20; 12:27; 15:44, 50; Rom. 6:13; Phil. 3:21; Sevenster, *Paul and Seneca*, pp. 77–81; Jacard, *Histoire sociale du travail*, pp. 102–12.

16. *Epistolae* 31.4–5; 44.1–4; *De brevitate vitae* 15.3. See also *Epistolae* 88.20, 28; 89.13; Sevenster, *Paul and Seneca*, p. 215.

humblest honest labor. The Bible was a radical document in respect to work.

Over the centuries the biblical motifs were overshadowed by other concerns. We cannot hope to do justice to all of these developments, so we will focus just on two of the most important figures—Augustine and Thomas Aquinas.

Augustine sought to come to grips with the entire life of the world about him as he sought to understand the relationship of the City of God to the City of Man. He had praise for the work of farmers, craftsmen, and even, on occasion, merchants. He certainly thought that "Christians will not refuse the discipline of this temporal life." However, he tended to view this life as only a *school* for life eternal. One analogy he used was that of a wayside inn: "Thou art passing on the journey thou hast begun, thou hast come, again to depart, not to abide . . . this life is but a wayside inn. Use [it] . . . with the purpose not of remaining but of leaving them behind." In this conception one could "use" *(uti)* worldly goods, but one could "enjoy" *(frui)* spiritual goods.[17]

Augustine distinguished between an "active life" *(vita activa)* and a "contemplative life" *(vita contemplativa)*. The contemplative life was akin to Aristotle's *bios politikos* and was largely derived from Greek and Roman thinking. The *vita activa* took in almost every kind of work, even including that of studying, preaching, and teaching, while the *vita contemplativa* was reflection and meditation upon God and his truth. While both of these kinds of life were good, the contemplative life was of a higher order. At times it might be necessary for one to have the active life, but, wherever possible, one should choose the other; "the one life is loved, the other endured." "The obligations of charity make us undertake righteous business *(negotium)*," but "if no one lays this burden upon us, we should give ourselves up to leisure *(otium)* to the perception and contemplation of truth."[18]

Thomas Aquinas also took the world and all its work with the

17. *De civitate dei* 1.29; 11.25; Herbert A. Deane, *The Political and Social Ideas of St. Augustine* (New York: Columbia University Press, 1963), pp. 44, 108ff.

18. Cuthbert Butler, *Western Mysticism: The Teaching of Augustine, Gregory and Bernard on Contemplation and the Contemplative Life*, 3d ed. (New York: Barnes and Noble, 1968), pp. 157–65; Arendt, *The Human Condition*, pp. 13, 15, 304, 376–77; "Sermon" 169.17; *De civitate dei* 11.16; 19.1, 2, 19; *Expositio in Psalmos* 69.7; *In Ioann. Evangel.* 6.25–26; *Tract in Ioann.* 124.5.

utmost seriousness. He was a member of a largely urban order, the Dominicans, and he sought to come to grips with all the manifestations of life about him, to point out the place of each human concern in the overarching of God's creation. For him the division of labor was a manifestation that all were members of the one body; he even compared God to a master craftsman.[19]

However, Thomas also used Augustine's distinction of the *vita contemplativa* and the *vita activa*. Although he gave everything its place, yet some things had a higher place than others. The *vita contemplativa* was "oriented to the eternal" whereas the *vita activa* was only because of the "necessities of the present life." The active life was connected only to the needs of the human body that men and animals had in common. It was good if it was necessary, but if one could stay alive without such work, then so much the better; it might even function only as a last resort. While both lives had their place, the active life was bound by necessity and only the contemplative life was truly free. In short, "the life of contemplation" was "simply better than the life of action."[20]

This sort of distinction formed the basic pattern of medieval Christianity. It resulted in a conception according to which the only true Christian calling, or at least the highest calling, was a priestly or monastic one. In fact the term *calling* or *vocation* was only used to refer to such pursuits. Karl Barth's summary was quite accurate:

> According to the view prevalent at the height of the high Middle ages [secular work] only existed to free for the work of their profession those who were totally and exclusively occupied in rendering true obedience for the salvation of each and all. There could be no question of "calling" for Christians in other professions.[21]

19. Cf. G. O'Brien, *An Essay on Medieval Economic Thinking* (London: Longmans, Green, 1920), p. 129; S. M. Killeen, *The Philosophy of Labour According to Thomas Aquinas* (Washington, D.C.: Catholic University of America, 1939).

20. *Summa theologiae* 2.2.179, 181 (1–4), 182 (1–2); *Expositio in Psalmos* 45.3; *Summa contra gentiles* 3.135; Arendt, *The Human Condition*, pp. 290, 303–4, 377.

21. Karl Barth, "Vocation," pp. 600ff. of vol. 3, part 4, of his *Church Dogmatics*, trans. A. T. Mackay et al. (Edinburgh: T. & T. Clark, 1961), p. 602; Th. Scharmann et al., "Beruf," in *Die Religion in Geschichte und Gegenwart*, edited by J. C. B. Mohr (Tübingen: J. C. B. Mohr, 1957), pp. 1071–80, 1078; K. Holl, "Die Geschichte des Worts 'Beruf,'" in his *Gesammelte Aufsätze zur Kirchengeschichte*, vol. 3 (Tübingen: J. C. B. Mohr, 1931), pp. 184–219, 199–200.

There were exceptions to this trend, the German mystics Meister Eckhart and Johann Tauler, and the English John Wyclif being the prime examples.[22] But each of these figures was regarded as mildly or outright heretical. Their unorthodox stance merely serves to throw into sharper focus the prevailing ethos of medieval Christianity.

The Reformation and Work

In the Reformation there was a very different outlook from the then existing Roman Catholic one. Almost without exception the Reformers maintained that all forms of work were of equal value and were equally pleasing to God. Indeed, one of the articles of heresy against William Tyndale, the major English Reformer who was executed for heresy in 1536, was that he taught: "There is no work better than another to please God; to pour water, to wash dishes, to be a souter (cobbler), or an apostle, all is one; to wash dishes and to preach is all one, as touching the deed, to please God." Tyndale was of the opinion that "in Christ we are all of one degree, without respect of persons." His fellow Reformer John Frith, executed in 1533, was of the same opinion: "How shalt thou learn to understand the Scripture, than by going about to fulfill that thou there readest? And if thou go about to fulfill it . . . then thou must work with thy hands, for that doth St. Paul teach thee."[23] The same views were the theme of the continental Reformation teaching. Luther taught that God in his providence had put every person in his place in society to do the work of that place:

> If you are a manual laborer, you find that the Bible has been put into your workshop, into your hand, into your heart. It teaches and preaches how you should treat your neighbour . . . just look at your tools . . . at your needle and thimble, your beer barrel, your

22. For Eckhart see Ray C. Petry, ed., *Late Medieval Mysticism* (Philadelphia: Westminster, 1957), pp. 193–99; for Tauler see *Oeuvres complètes*, 9 vols. (Paris: Tralin, 1911), 3:454–64; 4:126–47; for Wyclif see *Select English Works*, 3 vols. (Oxford: Oxford University Press, 1871), 3:130–34, 142–43, 148–49.
23. William Tyndale, "A Parable of the Wicked Mammon" (1527), in *Doctrinal Treatises and Portions of Holy Scripture* (Cambridge: Parker Society, 1848), pp. 98, 104; W. R. Jones, *The Tudor Commonwealth, 1529–1559* (London: Athlone, 1970), p. 68.

21

goods, your scales or yardstick or measure . . . and you will read this statement inscribed in them. Everywhere you look, it stares at you. . . . You have as many preachers as you have transactions, goods, tools and other equipment in your house and home.

Even Adam had "work to do, that is . . . plant the garden, cultivate and look after it." "Everything our bodies do, the external and the carnal, is and is called spiritual behaviour, if God's word is added to it and it is done in faith. There is therefore nothing which is so bodily, carnal and external that it does not become spiritual when it is done in the Word of God and faith." Luther's wicked jibe at the humanist Erasmus that he had no real sympathy with God's good creation and stared at the creatures "as a cow stares at a new gate" may not say much about Luther's knowledge of Erasmus, but it speaks volumes about his knowledge of cows![24]

Calvin was perhaps the strongest in his exhortations on work. Above all, he stressed *useful* work; his God was "not such as is imagined by the Sophists, vain, idle and almost asleep, but vigilant, efficacious, operative, and engaged in continual action." In his commentary on the parable of the talents (Luke 19:11–27), he broke away from previous interpretations which had understood the "talents" as spiritual gifts and graces. Calvin related the talents to everyday work and calling; the particular example he considered was trading *(negotiara)*. He stressed the concrete nature of these gifts and helped shape the modern meaning of the word *talent*. André Biéler, in his classic work on Calvin's social views, described Calvin's position thus:

> Companionship is completed in work and in the interplay of economic exchanges. Human fellowship is realized in relationships which flow from the division of labour wherein each person has been called of God to a particular and partial work which complements the work of others. The mutual exchange of goods and services is the concrete sign of the profound solidarity which unites humanity.[25]

24. Gustav Wingren, *Luther on Vocation* (Philadelphia: Muhlenberg, 1957), pp. 70–72; Paul Althaus, *The Ethics of Martin Luther* (Philadelphia: Muhlenberg, 1972), pp. 40, 101; *Luther's Works* (Philadelphia and St. Louis: Concordia and Muhlenberg, 1955–), 21:237; 31:360.

25. *Institutes* 1.16.3; Mario Miegge, *I Talenti Messi a Profitto* (Urbino: Argalia, 1969), pp. 7, 112–13; André Biéler, *La pensée économique et sociale de Calvin* (Geneva: Librairie de l'Université, 1961), p. 321.

There were certainly errors in the Reformers' views, as we shall see, but the general pattern of their teaching was essentially that of the New Testament: All work is equal in value; all our work is to be service to God; when done before the face of God, this world with its duties is our sphere of service.

It is hard to escape the impression that the followers of Augustine and Aquinas were to serve in the world only when necessary, that Luther's followers were ushered out to serve in the world, and that Calvin's followers were let loose to transform the world.

The Reformers' Confusion of Vocation, Work, and Job

While we have stressed the distinctiveness of the Reformation teaching on work and have maintained that the substance of what they taught was essentially biblical, it should not be thought that their views were without spot or wrinkle. In fact, many of our present problems stem from some of the Reformers' mistakes. I would like to focus on just one point: the confusion of vocation, work, and job.

One of the key texts in the Reformers' understanding of work was 1 Corinthians 7:20: "Abide in the calling in which you were called." Almost without exception they took the "calling" in this text to mean the works and estates that Christians were already in. Hence they taught that all persons should accept the place and station in society that they were in as the sphere where God had commanded them to work—in short, it was their calling. Luther often interchanged calling and social station (*Stand*). While Calvin was more open to changing work, he usually advised people to stay put unless they had "good grounds" and, hence, clearly related calling or vocation to a Christian's place in the social order and the economic division of labor.

Such an interpretation was a misreading of Paul unless he was using the word *calling (klēsis)* in a sense used nowhere else in his or any other Greek writings. It seems most likely that Paul was saying that circumcision or uncircumcision was relatively unimportant (vv. 17–19), that one's type of work was relatively unimportant (vv. 21–24), and that what was paramount was that people abide in the calling *as Christians.*

When the Reformers filtered their understanding of work

through their interpretation of this text, they sidetracked the biblical theme. A calling tended to be reduced to the activities required by being in a particular place in society. Thus to be a cobbler, a housewife, a husband, a preacher, or a farmer was a calling. Obedience in the world was focused in a particular type of work for each person.[26] The overall result of this was that Christians were directed to serve God in the world, but the world and its "callings" were taken for granted. The renewing implications of Christian vocation were suppressed in favor of a quiescence and passivity before the social order. Christians were to be farmers, housewives, and merchants, but never really asked whether being such was really such a fruitful and just service under the prevailing conditions.

Over the next 150 years, with the growth of *jobs* (i.e., paid work), the idea of calling became even narrower. Calling then tended to mean just a type of *job*. One result of this was that unpaid work was downgraded. "Real" work was paid; activities like comforting the heartbroken or visiting the sick were all right, but they were a bit lightweight if they didn't bring in the bacon. Women still had something of a vocation in housekeeping and parenting, but that was somehow not up to par with "real" work. Men's vocations were their jobs, trades, and professions; other things might be good but were, with the exception of piety, optional.

Another result of the fact that a calling *was* a job was that, as work structures changed, the content of a calling changed as well. To be sure, Christians were urged to be honest and earnest, but the actual *content* of the work they were doing was never open to question. This eventually resulted in the sort of teaching offered by the late-seventeenth-century Puritan Richard Steele:

> Let (a man) be never so active out of his sphere, he will be at a great
> loss, if he do not keep his own vineyard and mind his own business
> . . . it is not our sin that we do not supply another's negligence, by
> doing that which belongs not in our place . . . there is poor com-

26. Cf. Wingren, *Luther on Vocation*, p. 64; Calvin's *Commentary on the First Epistle to the Corinthians*, edited by David W. Torrance and Thomas F. Torrance, translated by John W. Frazer (Grand Rapids: Eerdmans, 1960), pp. 150–55; *Institutes* 3.10.6.

fort in suffering for doing that which was not the work of our place and calling. . . .[27]

The general maxims of an individualistic and secularizing age now provided almost the sole content of a Christian calling. While it is true that such a tendency was not developed in the Reformers themselves, they sowed the seeds which ultimately grew up and almost strangled any biblical conception of vocation.

The Age of Enlightenment

Radical changes in thought and action swept Europe during the turbulent years of the sixteenth and seventeenth centuries, ultimately giving rise to what is commonly referred to as the age of Enlightenment, which led to the industrial revolution.

Adam Smith (1723–1790), the world's first great economist, lived at the very beginning of the industrial revolution. How vastly different his world was from that of the Reformation two hundred years earlier or, for that matter, from that of the late Middle Ages! The medieval doctors of theology exalted spiritual work, relegated manual labor to a place of secondary importance, and frowned on all economic motives. Calvin and Luther restored work to its proper place in creation as a God-given vocation, but emphasized the need for a God-centered life of service. Even more than their medieval predecessors, they condemned the desire to become rich in this world, and they did not hesitate to condemn and discipline those who pursued material gain out of economic self-interest.

Not so Adam Smith and his contemporaries. Renaissance faith in the autonomy of man had rapidly conquered the lingering medieval patterns of thought in the West. God was no longer regarded as the living God asking people to serve him and one another. Instead, God had become some distant being who, after creating the world, had retired, leaving man the task to explore

27. I [Paul Marshall] have traced the post-Reformation evolution of calling as job in "The Calling: Secularization and Economics in the Seventeenth Century," a paper presented in 1978 at the annual meeting of the Canadian Political Science Association in London, Ontario; and in "John Locke: Between God and Mammon," *Canadian Journal of Political Science* 12 (1979): 73–96.

and define the laws of nature. In fulfilling this task, man is guided not by God's revelation, but by reason, that inner light common to all men. This new religion—called deism—is fundamental to Enlightenment developments.

Whereas the medieval fathers and the Reformers taught that we must refrain from merely seeking ourselves, Smith elevated the principle of self-interest to the motivating force in society. "It is not from the benevolence of the butcher, the brewer, or the baker that we expect our dinner," he said, "but from their regard to their own interest. We address ourselves, not to their humanity but to their self-love, and never talk to them of our own necessities but of their advantages."[28] But how is it possible that a society in which everyone is engaged in a mad scramble after self-interest does not fall apart and end up in anarchy? According to Smith the market prevents this catastrophe. The supposed "invisible hand" of the market will see to it that each gets his due. The laws of the market will show us how self-interest will result in competition, and competition, in turn, will result in the provision of those goods society wants at prices society is prepared to pay. For example, if a glove manufacturer out of self-interest would raise the price of his product above that of his competitors, people automatically would stop buying his gloves. The market would thus force the price down. However, if everyone would want to buy gloves, a shortage of gloves would result, causing the price to rise. Then manufacturers of other products—shoes, for instance—would feel the pinch and would also begin to make gloves. Thus the glove market would soon become saturated, causing an automatic decrease in the price. In turn, this would lead to a decrease in the production of gloves and a greater production of another commodity. In other words, the forces of supply and demand make the market a self-regulating mechanism.

The same law of supply and demand applies, according to Smith, to the population. Workers for him are commodities to be produced in accordance with demand. If wages are high, the number of working people multiplies; if wages fall, this number decreases. In Smith's days infant mortality was shockingly high. "It is not uncommon in the Highlands of Scotland," says Smith,

28. Adam Smith, *The Wealth of Nations* (1776; New York: Modern Library, 1937), p. 14.

"for a mother who has borne twenty children not to have two alive." Throughout England half the children lived only to the age of nine or ten. Higher wages, however, will bring about better social conditions resulting in a lower death rate. But then, says Smith, the market mechanism takes over. Heilbroner summarized his arguments as follows: "Just as higher prices on the market will bring about a larger production of gloves and the larger number of gloves in turn press down the higher prices of gloves, so higher wages will bring about a larger number of workers, and the increase in their numbers will set up a reverse pressure on the level of their wages. Population, like glove production, is a self-curing disease—as far as wages are concerned."[29] In the fantasy world of Adam Smith, all will be well as long as no one tampers with the market mechanism. Don't try to do good, he says; let good emerge as the byproduct of selfishness.

It is not surprising that the real world showed a different picture. Work was not motivated by a Protestant work ethic derived largely from Calvin, as Max Weber asserted in his famous *The Protestant Ethic and the Spirit of Capitalism*. Rather, it was controlled by a humanist work ethic which had its roots in the Renaissance faith that nothing can stop autonomous man from conquering the world by means of his own genius. This work ethic was based on the so-called iron laws of nature, not on God's law of love.

Entrepreneurs adopted the notion developed by John Locke, Adam Smith, David Ricardo, and others that the real value of every commodity is its labor value. Therefore, the only value of the worker is his capacity to perform work; other than that he has no value. It is important to note here that this idea still prevails strongly in today's labor relations.

Entrepreneurs also readily assented to Smith's dictum that the market—especially the labor market—should be left alone, unhindered by governmental influence.

Smith died in 1790 during the early stages of the industrial revolution, and his lessons had been learned well by the industrialists, who changed the face of the earth. As is well known, this was accompanied by the most inhuman situations. Already in

29. Robert L. Heilbroner, *The Worldly Philosophers* (New York: Simon and Schuster, 1953), pp. 59, 59–60.

Smith's days working conditions were terrible. In the coal mines of Durham and Northumberland, men and women worked together, stripped to the waist, under the most inhuman conditions. Children of seven years and older, who never saw daylight during the winter months, slaved away to augment the miners' pitiful wages. Pregnant women drew coal cars like horses and even gave birth in the dark, black caverns of the mines.

After the great inventions of the latter half of the eighteenth century, industrialization accelerated and England became the industrial heartland of the world. The misery which then descended on the workers defies description and is virtually unparalleled in history. Workdays of fourteen and sixteen hours were normal. Little children were carried to the factories by their parents as early as four o'clock in the morning and were often tied to the machines, lest they should fall asleep or run away. They were subjected to brutal treatment by foremen and managers, whose authority was unquestioned.

The urge to obtain wealth became the driving force behind the industrial development. The means to that end was work. During the first half of the nineteenth century, the work ethic of incessant hard labor began to assume the nature of a religion. By 1851 the Great Exhibition in the Crystal Palace in London was set up as a showpiece of what work and industry had accomplished. On that occasion *The Economist* printed the following telling editorial:

> Without pretending on the present occasion to appreciate all the bearings of this Exhibition . . . we may briefly notice its moral significance. The Queen of the mightiest empire of the globe—the empire in which industry is the most successfully cultivated, and in which its triumphs have been greatest—was fittingly occupied in consecrating the temple erected to its honour. . . . The contrast and the change we have noticed . . . the former disdain . . . for humble industry, and the present honour it bestows, telling of a future when the hand or the skill of the labourer shall be held in still higher honour . . . are convincing proofs of the moral improvements already made; and they give us irresistible assurances that a yet higher destiny awaits our successors even on earth.[30]

30. *The Economist*, 3 May 1851, p. 474.

The Deification of Work

It often happens that disciples, thinking they are following in the footsteps of the master, end up saying and doing things which are quite contrary to the master's teachings. This can clearly be seen in the followers of John Calvin.

English and American Puritans, as well as German and Dutch pietists, claiming to be children and heirs of the Reformation, developed a work ethic which deviated sharply from Calvin's ideas. For the Puritans, work, even hard labor, was a divine mandate, whereas leisure was frowned upon as idleness. Success was often seen as a sign of God's favor and the road to success was thrift and hard work. For the Puritans shalom was not God's gift which must permeate our entire life. Shalom was reward for diligence. Their interpretation of the fourth commandment placed more emphasis on "six days shalt thou labor" than on "remember the sabbath (rest) day." They observed the letter of the law to the point that the Puritan settlers of New England spent most of the Sunday sitting silently at home with blinds drawn to keep the sunlight out.

In eighteenth- and nineteenth-century Protestantism there was a strong tendency to identify with the humanist work ethic. John Wesley believed that hard work and a frugal lifestyle were beneficent for the soul. Spurgeon taught that labor was a shield against the temptations of the devil. To prove his point he reminded his audience that in the Bible God appeared to people while they were working: Moses was tending the flock, Gideon was threshing the corn, Elisha was plowing the field, and the disciples were out fishing. (The well-known Dutch theologian and writer Okke Jager makes the ironical remark that Spurgeon conveniently forgot to mention the times God appeared to people in their sleep.)

Did not Calvin teach that to work was to fulfill one's calling and that thrift was to be preferred over extravagance? And did not the new work ethic also urge people to produce for the ultimate good of all? Here, it seems, lies much of the reason why capitalism and Christianity are so often identified and why so many Protestant Christians in North America are such ardent supporters of the free-enterprise system.

There is some truth to Max Weber's assertion that the Protestant work ethic was linked to Calvinism, although he greatly overstates his case by tracing the argument back to Calvin himself. Calvin's view of labor and leisure was derived more from the promise of shalom God's people may have in Christ. One should note that the Heidelberg Catechism, written by some of Calvin's immediate disciples, explains the fourth commandment in terms of the true sabbath (rest) for all of our lives.

Marxists are also guilty of deviating from their master's teachings. In his early writings Marx taught that nature will ultimately attain its human destiny and man will reach his natural goal by means of human labor. Only through work does man become fully human. However, Marx also made allowance for man as a multidimensional being whose activities go much beyond hard work. Marx foresaw a society in which the worker could spend much of his time in leisure and would also be able to perform varying tasks.

However, Marx's friend and associate Friedrich Engels, who came from a pietist (Puritan) family, and many of his followers increasingly glorified work as an end in itself. As a result, in Marxist countries the worker and his work have taken on a religious significance. Marxists know of only two classes: the working class (proletariat) and the ruling class (bourgeoisie). The former constitutes the elect, the latter the reprobate. Between them runs the line between good and evil. To belong to the working class means sharing in the way of redemption, while to have one's roots in ruling-class circles almost equals being guilty of original sin. Solzhenitsyn, describing the Stalinist purges in his *Gulag Archipelago*, states that the interrogators and prosecutors never asked whether the accused was guilty of crimes against socialism, but whether he *could* have been guilty. And the answer to that question depended to a large extent on the defendant's background, i.e., to what class his parents belonged. Solzhenitsyn also states that the authorities in the labor camps of the *Gulag* considered hard work, even inhumanly severe labor, as a *purifying* experience. Such work would have a *cleansing* effect on the polluted mind of the inmate, and would prepare him again for his task in the socialist order.

The Fall of the Idol

One of the driving forces behind the industrial development of the nineteenth century was the desire to become wealthy. Although the desire to gain personal wealth played a large role (note, for instance, that many entrepreneurs in Europe and America became immensely rich), the overall goal was to become wealthy as a nation, for this, in turn, would be to the benefit of all. This absolutization of wealth and property has been a characteristic of Western civilization over the past 250 years. The dominant motives of our culture consist no longer in the service of God and neighbor, but in self-fulfillment and the acquisition of material things.

The desire to accumulate wealth and property had a demeaning influence on man and thing alike. For it meant that work, the worker, and the product of his hand ultimately became debased.

To see this more clearly, let us take another look at the era preceding the Enlightenment. In the medieval order the craftsman had a certain status. His position was an honorable one. Although his pay may not have been great, it must be remembered that high wages were not the goal of life. Society was static; the aim of life was how to attain the kingdom of heaven, how to be saved for a life hereafter for which this life was but a portal. Work was executed in a leisurely manner without the feverish pace so familiar to us. It was focused on making products (things) that had meaning transcending earthly life. Numerous artifacts of those days still exist, and they attest to the fact that a thing was much more than a mere utensil, something to be used, worn out, and discarded. An object was made, used, and handled as having a value that points to God. One sees this probably best expressed in cathedrals and public buildings erected during that period. The same reverence is found in the articles and edifices of the time of the Reformation.

The Enlightenment, with its emphasis on autonomous man, placed man in the center of life and relegated God and his kingdom to a place of secondary importance. It is not surprising that this shift in the focus of life reflects itself in man's products, in his work, and in his view of the worker. With the advent of mass production, the product became more and more a utensil whose purpose it was to serve man rather than God. Industrial production also diminished the role of craftsmanship; in fact, almost eliminated it. Work itself, from being meaningful, became meaningless. Thus the product, the work, and the worker were all robbed of their deeper meaning and were subjected to a utilitarian point of view.

31

It is significant to note in this context how Jeremy Bentham (1748–1832), father of utilitarianism, defined the norm for life: "Nature has placed mankind under the governance of two sovereign masters, *pain* and *pleasure*. It is for them alone to point out what we ought to do, as well as to determine what we shall do. On the one hand the standard of right and wrong, on the other the chain of causes and effects, are fastened to their throne. They [pain and pleasure] govern us in all we do, in all we say, in all we think; every effort we can make to throw off our subjection will serve but to demonstrate and confirm it." "Pleasure," says Bentham, "is the only good . . . and pain is the only evil."[31] These, in other words, are the new norms for all of human behavior, and they replace the biblical norms for good and evil, right and wrong. Economists and industrialists alike adopted Bentham's dictum and began to consider the possession of consumption goods as a pleasure (hence good) and the performance of work as a pain (hence evil). Obviously this notion is diametrically opposed to what the Bible teaches about these matters. It frequently warns against the possession of many material things, and it upholds work as inherently human and part of God's mandate for man.

From being deified, work as such now became a pain and fell from its newly gained pedestal of worship.

Study Questions

1. Summarize the main differences between Greek and Roman attitudes toward work and the biblical principles discussed in chapter 1.
2. The apostle Paul has sometimes been described as a Christian stoic. How accurate do you think that view is?
3. In what ways did pre-Reformation principles distort biblical teaching on work?
4. What is the relevance of the Reformers' teaching on work in today's society?
5. What are the positive and negative aspects of the "Puritan work ethic" as described in the section entitled "The Deification of Work"?

31. Jeremy Bentham, *Introduction to the Principles of Morals and Legislation*, edited by Laurence J. Lafleur (New York: Hafner, 1948), pp. 1–2.

Creatively Choosing a Career   3

We are hardly breaking new ground when we say that the choice of a career is one of the major decisions of life. From the perennial childhood question, "What are you going to do when you grow up," through adolescent concern that "I can't decide what to do with my life," to midlife musing, "I wonder if it's time for a change," much of human development is bound up with career-related decisions. As Christians we believe that God is interested in every aspect of our lives and has provided us with gifts and motivations to use in his service. We also believe that God offers guidance to us through his Holy Spirit, through Scripture, and through his people. This faith in a purposeful and planning God is the context in which Christians are to approach vocational choice.

We should not abuse the principle of guidance, however, by viewing it as a process of discovering the single divine blueprint in which only one career path will accord with God's plan. The biblical teaching on calling has too often been interpreted as a "divine blueprint," an approach Martin E. Clark seeks to correct in his book *Choosing Your Career.*

Romans 12:2 urges us not to be conformed to this world but to be transformed by the renewing of our minds. Being true to this in the modern world of work may well involve the consideration of radically different career paths based upon sacrificial service and simple lifestyle rather than upon upward mobility and material prosperity.

The Call[1]

Does God call us to specific careers?

Most secular textbooks on career development that include a discussion of various career theories mention a "divine selection theory." Usually labeled "antiquated" and assigned to a Middle Ages mentality, this theory proposes that each person is both chosen for a career and informed of his fate by a supreme Being. Naturally this approach is ridiculed widely today because it is seen as too deterministic and it supposedly robs us of autonomy in career choice.

Ironically each career theory proposed in place of divine selection represents a more severe form of determinism. Theories of career choice have been focused at heredity, socio-economic factors, psychological limits, and the developmental process, and all of these propose one type of determinism or another. The ridicule focused on divine selection, then, comes not from its determinism, per se. Rather, it arises from the assumption that God does not exist, or at least is not personally active, and that man is the sole determiner and measure of all things.

We should not be surprised when a culture that has tried to excise all consideration of God from its thinking rebels against the idea that God would be involved in career choice. As Christians we may not agree completely with the divine-selection theory as stated above, but we do believe in the existence of an orderly, personal God.

Since God is orderly, we can safely conclude that his plan includes his children, those who have been saved by his grace through faith in Jesus Christ. It is inconceivable that God would have an orderly plan and fail to include in it the work of his creatures, especially those whom he has redeemed. That God has a plan for our lives follows naturally from the fact that he is orderly.

1. This section consists of excerpts from Martin E. Clark, *Choosing Your Career: The Christian's Decision Manual* (Phillipsburg, N.J.: Presbyterian and Reformed, 1981), pp. 89–98.

Also, since God is personal, we can safely conclude that he has a personal interest and concern for each of us. He has personally been involved in our lives—forming us, developing us, saving us, leading us, gifting us. It is unthinkable that he would not guide us in such a crucial matter as career choice, but rather leave that to some impersonal, fatalistic force. And it is also unthinkable that a personal God would have a plan for our lives and wish to conceal it from us.

How, then, does God inform us of his will for us? The term *call* has been used to denote the process in which he enlightens us regarding his plan for our careers. And sometimes a "call" is limited only to professional ministry careers (e.g., pastor, missionary), giving the impression that those in other careers have had no calling.

We are then faced with at least two pressing questions: "What is a 'call'?" and "How do I know if I have been called?" The discussion that follows may not answer these questions directly, but it will at least provide a framework for considering them.

The Call to Salvation

The vast majority of Scripture passages that speak of God's "call" refer to his call to salvation and to holy living. Concerning our salvation, for example, the Bible states that we are *called* out of darkness into his light (1 Peter 2:9), *called* to repentance (Acts 2:38–39), *called* by the gospel (2 Thess. 2:14), *called* into fellowship with Jesus Christ (1 Cor. 1:9), *called* into the body of Christ (Col. 3:15), *called* into his kingdom (1 Thess. 2:12), and *called* to eternal life (1 Tim. 6:12, Heb. 9:15).

As Christians we are *called* to be saints (1 Cor. 1:2), denoting not only our salvation but also holy living following our conversion. A call to holiness should be expected when we consider the fact that it is the Holy One who calls us (1 Peter 1:15).

Every Christian, then, has received God's call. Without it we would never be saved (Rom. 8:30). But this *call* concerns salvation, not career choice. Perhaps this biblical emphasis on the call to salvation should remind us that God's will for our lives focuses much more on the people we *are*, rather than on how we earn a living.

The Call to Christian-Service Careers

The question "Are you called?" is normally asked of persons

planning to enter Christian-service careers, especially within evangelical circles. Most must assert and somehow prove this calling before being ordained or commissioned for missionary service.

The expression *full-time Christian service* is not used here because every Christian is called to serve Christ all the time regardless of his career. In place of this inadequate expression, we will refer to "Christian-service careers" and "professional-ministry careers." Both of these terms more adequately convey the concept of serving Christ in a vocational manner. While every Christian is to serve Christ and minister to fellow believers, some are called to do so in a career sense, and they earn their living by their ministries. These we are calling "Christian-service careers." "Secular careers" are those in which one's living is earned by functions other than ministry. While it is probably impossible to draw a clear line between the two, the Scripture does indicate that there is some difference and that this difference involves the matter of earning the living (1 Cor. 9:14). "Secular careers" are neither less spiritual nor less sacred than Christian-service careers, for the spirituality of one's work is determined not by the content of the work but by the spirituality of the worker.

Although the biblical passages are relatively scarce, there is sufficient revelation to warrant the assertion that a call should precede entry to a Christian-service career. The Old Testament priests and prophets occupied their positions by God's choice, not by their own selection. He was speaking of priests when the writer of Hebrews stated, "No one takes the honor to himself, but receives it when he is called by God, even as Aaron was" (5:4 [NASB]). Amos recounts his own call to the prophetic ministry in this way: "I am a herdsman and a grower of sycamore figs. But the LORD took me from following the flock and . . . said to me, 'Go prophesy to My people Israel'" (7:14–15 [NASB]). Those who represented God did so at his initiative and direction, not their own.

In the New Testament Jesus chose the disciples who would become the apostles (Luke 6:13ff.). While each one had an eagerness to follow him, no one became a disciple/apostle by volunteering. Rather, they were specifically called by Jesus Christ to their ministries. Similarly Paul speaks of being *called* to be an apostle (Rom. 1:1; 1 Cor. 1:1), and within that office, *called* to preach (Acts 16:10). He was "appointed a preacher and an apostle and a teacher" (2 Tim. 1:11 [NASB]). Consequently he felt constrained by

God to such an extent that he exclaimed, "Woe is me if I do not preach the gospel" (1 Cor. 9:16 [NASB]). Paul's calling came, of course, through the extraordinary means of a vision (Acts 9), a means God used only occasionally in Bible times and not at all today.

Most of the biblical data concerning the call to ministry pertains to offices no longer functioning (priest, prophet, apostle). Consequently the concepts we have of current calls to ministry are usually the applications we make from the formerly functioning offices to the presently functioning ones. We may infer that God selects evangelists and pastor/teachers today as he did the prophets and apostles, since he lists them together as his gifts to the church (Eph. 4:11). He does "send" persons to preach (Rom. 10:15), and he plans for those who preach the gospel to make their living by their ministry (1 Cor. 9:14).

Some argument for a call might rightly be made from the nature of Christian-service careers. To represent the Lord without his call to do so would be presumptuous. Wagner says: "It is incongruous to think that an ambassador would go to a country as a representative of his homeland without being sent. To take such a position would be unthinkable. This is even more true in the ministry. . . . To go, without being sent, is to walk in failure."[2] But the Scripture simply does not emphasize the calling of pastor/teachers as much as it does the calling of persons to the offices of priest, prophet, and apostle (and it makes no mention whatever of calls to non-preaching ministries such as medical missions, Christian-school teaching, writing).

Does this mean that pastor/teachers and evangelists need not be "called" of God? Does it mean that medical missionaries and Christian educators are not called? The biblical evidence, though not abundant, gives sufficient basis for believing that God *does call* persons into his service. We are mistaken if we try to justify present-day "calls" by equating present ministries with the apostolic and prophetic offices (e.g., missionary = apostle; pastor = prophet), because these offices were to serve the church only in its infancy (Eph. 2:20). A preferable approach would be to define this calling as *God's personal guidance through which he enlightens us*

2. Charles U. Wagner, *The Pastor: His Life and Work* (Schaumberg, Ill.: Regular Baptist, 1976), p. 1.

regarding his plan for our lives. While none of his guidance will ever contradict his Word, it is probably unnecessary to pin every aspect of his plan for every one of his children to a specific Bible verse. And so we will focus on this guidance rather than trying to find specific verses to justify calls to every type of ministry.

How, then, can we know if we are called into some Christian-service career? We must admit that the New Testament does not describe the mechanics of a call, nor does it give a concise checklist for recognizing calls. The following suggestions, then, are based in part on human experience in addition to divine revelation, but perhaps they still have some value in that God may choose to grant similar experiences in calling people to similar tasks.

The first indication usually is a consciousness within our own minds that God desires this for us. Lloyd-Jones has stated: "A call generally starts in the form of a consciousness within one's own spirit, some disturbance in the realm of the spirit, that your mind is being directed . . . it is God dealing with you, and God acting upon you by His Spirit; it is something you become aware of rather than something you do."[3] This awareness is more a mental conviction than an emotional upheaval. The work of God within the mind produces both a desire and a sense of necessity. We should expect him to give us a desire for ministry if that is his plan. Paul wrote, "If a man *desire* the office of a bishop, he desireth a good work" (1 Tim. 3:1 [KJV]). As this desire matures, it strengthens into the kind of constraint Paul felt in his ministry: "I am under compulsion; for woe is me if I do not preach the gospel" (1 Cor. 9:16 [NASB]). The guidance of God is recognized as a "divine initiative, a solemn communication of the divine will . . . which leaves a man no alternative."[4]

Another indication of God's leadership into a Christian-service career is the insight and testimony of godly persons. For instance, the church members at Antioch recognized God's call of Barnabas and Saul to missionary service at least as quickly as the missionaries themselves did. This confirmation apparently was based not on some mysterious hunches, but on an evaluation of

---

3. D. Martyn Lloyd-Jones, *Preaching and Preachers* (Grand Rapids: Zondervan, 1972), p. 104.

4. J. H. Jowett, *The Preacher: His Life and Work* (New York: Harper, 1912), p. 19.

service already performed for the cause of Christ (Acts 13:1–3). If an inclination toward ministry is not verified by at least some godly acquaintances, a "call" should be doubted.

Since ministry serves to bring people into a relationship with God, we might expect called persons to have a right relationship themselves with God and with others. It is doubtful that God would press into his service one who despised him or his Word. A desire to know God and to handle his Word competently should be expected in the life of one called (as in every Christian's life). Those in the early church who were in career ministries purposed to devote themselves "to prayer, and to the ministry of the word" (Acts 6:4 [NASB]). A call to ministry is a call to study.

Similarly a right relationship with others is essential, and many of the personal qualifications listed for pastors are aimed at good interpersonal relations (1 Tim. 3; Titus 1). While not expecting everyone's love, understanding, or approval, one called into a ministry career will have a genuine concern for others. Lloyd-Jones writes: "The true call always includes a concern about others, an interest in them, a realization of their lost estate and condition, and a desire to do something about them, and to tell them the message and point them to the way of salvation. This is an essential part of the call; and it is important, particularly as a means whereby we may check ourselves."[5]

A call to the pastorate in particular must involve a serious examination of and commitment to the qualifications for pastors outlined in 1 Timothy 3 and Titus 1. Failure to meet these qualifications exempts one from pastoral office, no matter how strongly he may feel called! It may be noteworthy that "feeling called" is *not* listed among pastoral qualifications in either 1 Timothy or Titus. This omission does not mean a call is unnecessary. It probably indicates that these qualifications are criteria for determining whether one is called. While there is no concise checklist for determining a call, these qualifications probably are as close to being such a list as anything we have. Interestingly these criteria focus on personal traits and interpersonal relationships more than on specific aptitudes. The only vocational aptitude listed is the ability to teach. Spiritual maturity is emphasized, along with personal traits that demonstrate this matu-

5. Lloyd-Jones, *Preaching and Preachers*, pp. 104–5.

rity. Right relationships within both family and community are likewise emphasized. Consideration of these lists of qualifications will likely produce a sense of unworthiness or insufficiency, but we should be reminded that God promises growth and development when we follow him faithfully.

Spiritual gifts can serve as reliable indicators of a call to professional ministry since they are God-given abilities for service. The presence or absence of these gifts can therefore indicate appropriate roles within the church. Pastors, in particular, should have the gift of pastoring, which involves a spiritual protection and nurture of other believers. Additionally the qualifications and office description given to the pastorate in the New Testament would require at least the gifts of teaching, exhortation, and administration, and probably evangelism and helps also. Similarly other Christian-service careers require specific spiritual gifts, and if these are not present, at least in undeveloped form, a call should be doubted.

If God seems to direct us into a career of ministry, then we should examine not only the inward, subjective leading, but also the outward, objective facts. Some of the following questions may prove helpful in determining God's call.

Subjective criteria:

Do I think I am called?
Do I desire this ministry?
Do I feel I *must* be involved in this ministry?

Objective criteria:

Do I meet the appropriate qualifications?
Do I have confirmation from other believers?
Do I have the necessary spiritual gifts?
Do I have a genuine concern for other people?

Such an examination can assure us that we are placing appropriate emphasis on both subjective and objective aspects of our decision.

And since both subjective and objective aspects are involved, a call from God does not mean that the investigative and decision-making processes outlined earlier are unnecessary. A call does not decrease the necessity of knowing about ourselves; if anything, it increases the urgency of self-understanding. Neither does a call render unnecessary an understanding of what is involved in different ministry careers. Certainly a proper decision-making process is imperative in order to determine if one is truly called, and also to ascertain the nature and direction of the call. To say, therefore, "I can't be bothered with making career decisions because I have been called" is to take a shortsighted approach which shows a lack of understanding both of a "calling" and of career decision making. The career decision process outlined earlier is appropriate for those who "feel called." It will assist in determining, clarifying, and responding to the call.

We have already seen that the call to a Christian-service career is neither mysterious nor irrational. The Scripture records visions and other miraculous events connected with calling persons to offices that operated prior to the completion of Scripture (priests, prophets, apostles, and Old Testament leaders like Moses). *Nowhere* are we told that his calling of persons to continuing offices (e.g., pastor/teacher, missionary/evangelist, deacon) was accompanied by such supernatural signs and wonders, even in New Testament times! And *nowhere* are we told to expect such signs. What we should expect, however, are (1) God's equipping by granting grace for meeting biblical qualifications, (2) the Spirit's gifting for accomplishing the calling, and (3) God's implanting of a desire for ministry. In fact, many testify that their calling was not a sudden, spectacular event, but a gradually deepening conviction and a process in which God's work in their life was progressively clarified.

Calls to Other Careers

While the Scriptures give evidence that God calls persons into Christian-service careers, it does not use the same terminology regarding other careers. Paul was called to be an apostle, for instance, but although he was also a tentmaker, he does not say he was "called" to tentmaking. Similarly God's selection of priests and prophets receives emphasis, while we don't customarily read of him "calling" people to farming or to business. This difference has led to two common mistakes: (1) mystifying the call to Christian service so that it is encased with awe and exempted from rational decision making; (2) assigning all other careers to a non-call, non-spiritual status.

We have used the word *call* to describe the process whereby

God enlightens us regarding his plan for our careers. When understood in this sense, we see that God's guidance into other careers is just as much a "calling" as is his leading into professional ministry. While the outcomes may be quite different, the process is probably similar in both cases. Both require considerable prayer and trust in God for his guidance. Both should involve a rigorous self-examination as well as a thorough study of alternatives, evaluated by a scripturally-based value system. Both should seek to utilize the appropriate gifts and talents placed in the life by God. Both should include the strong, inward conviction that one is in the plan of God, doing God's will from the heart.

While many Christian accountants, homemakers, coal miners, and policemen may not refer to their careers as "callings," if they are pursuing their careers with assurance they are in God's plan, they have as much right to consider their careers "callings" as anyone else. In fact the word *vocation* is taken from the Latin *vocatio*, meaning "calling." Whoever speaks of his "vocation," therefore, is acknowledging his "calling." The Christian who is faithfully walking with his Lord acknowledges that his vocation (calling) has come from God, not from himself or from his world or from blind fate.

While the Christian fireman or nurse or scientist may not be able to justify his profession by pointing to a specific verse in the Bible, he can be assured that he is in God's plan as a result of God's personal leading. If we mistakenly think of his leading or call as a sudden, spectacular event, few of us will ever consider ourselves called to secular careers. But God's leading is normally neither sudden nor spectacular. His leading usually occurs on a day-by-day basis, teaching us about his work in our lives and guiding us through our experiences. Receiving God's guidance, like all of the Christian life, is not as much sudden spurts as it is consistent, faithful living.

Higher Callings, Lower Callings

Sermons meant to challenge people to enter Christian-service careers frequently refer to these careers as "God's highest calling." While usually not stated, the clear implication is that other careers are lower, and therefore somewhat inferior, callings.

The Scripture does present Christian service as a high calling. The pastoral office, for instance, is described as a "fine work" (1 Tim. 3:1 [NASB]), and being placed in the ministry requires evidence of faithfulness (1 Tim. 1:12). There should be no question that ministering the Word of God to people constitutes a high calling and that offices within the church involve considerable responsibility and authority.

As high a calling as the ministry is, however, we simply cannot support from Scripture a division between higher and lower callings. Rather, we see just the opposite in Scripture. When we study the biblical value of work, we see that God values all types of careers. A recognition that God is sovereign in dispensing gifts, abilities, limitations, and interests, reminds us that he guides his people into many different careers. Following his leadership and fulfilling his plan is a genuinely spiritual endeavor, regardless of the vocation involved. Ultimately a division between higher and lower callings reflects on the person of God, for after all, he is the One doing the calling.

Unfortunately the appeals to "God's highest calling," though well intentioned, can have sinful effects. These appeals can engender pride, as an artificial hierarchy is erected among Christians, some of whom are "higher" than others. Even the fact that church offices can involve authority does not create the hierarchy which places some people "higher" than others. Also, appeals to "God's highest calling" can coerce sensitive believers into Christian-service careers apart from God's leadership, simply because they mistakenly think they cannot experience God's best or his blessing otherwise. Further, these appeals frequently intimidate faithful Christians who have conscientiously followed God's leadership into secular careers.

Rather than thinking of higher and lower callings, we should recognize that any calling from God is a high calling, simply because he made it. The determining factor is not the content of the call, but the One who made it and the faithfulness of the one receiving it. If there is such a thing as a "lower calling," it is a career chosen out of a wrong attitude or in rebellion against God's leading. And again the determining factor is not the career itself, but the wrong attitude and unfaithfulness of the person.

When we believe in a personal, orderly God, we assume that he will work directly with us in granting guidance. God specifically chooses, prepares, and calls those whom he wishes to be in Christian-service careers. And since this choice, preparation, and guidance reflects his nature, he works in much the same manner in leading Christians into secular careers. The involvement of the eternal God, the Lord of heaven and earth, in guiding us in career choices constitutes those careers as high callings, regardless of the careers themselves.

So Who Wants to Be Upwardly Mobile?

Is it time to lay the "Yuppie" label to rest? Perhaps the term has been overused to the point of becoming a cliché. Despite the tiredness of the term, however, the ethos it represents is alive and well. The ideals centering around the goal of upward mobility form the counterculture to the counterculture, a generational statement expressed in the language of conformity rather than that of rebellion. Like their predecessors in the 1960s and 1970s, today's college students and graduates have a message to proclaim. But the slogan that summarizes a generation has changed from the anger of "Smash the system" and the plea of "Make love not war" to the confidence of "You can have it all."

The confidence may be a facade, a distorted attempt to compensate for the uncertainties and insecurities of the nuclear age—just so much whistling in the dark. If the ethos of upward mobility is indeed based upon insecurity or, alternatively, upon the idolization of materialism, then it would seem to be in glaring contradiction to the Christian message of hope on the one hand and detachment from earthly treasure on the other. The extraordinary truth of the matter, however, is that we are witnessing a widescale capitulation within the Christian community to the ideals of upward mobility, an insidious sacrilizing of a secular vision.

This unholy alliance, which in previous centuries would have been labeled a heresy, is humorously characterized by a poem which appeared in the *Washington Post:*

> Now I lay me down to sleep
> I pray my Cuisinart to keep
> I pray my stocks are on the rise
> And that my analyst is wise
> That all the wine I sip is white
> And that my hot tub's watertight
> That racquetball won't get too tough
> That all my sushi's fresh enough
> I pray my cordless phone still works

> That my career won't lose its perks
> My microwave won't radiate
> My condo won't depreciate
> I pray my health club doesn't close
> And that my money market grows
> If I go broke before I wake
> I pray my Volvo they won't take.

Behind this playful portrait in prayer lies a real set of expectations and values. Such a value system embodies a particular view of work and needs to be assessed on the basis of the biblical principles we outlined in chapter 1. Christians have been widely influenced by the tendency to view career as a vehicle for self-advancement, the acquisition of wealth, and the attainment of personal status. It is as if the apostle Paul had urged us, "Be not transformed by the renewing of your minds, but be conformed to this world."

Let us examine some creative Christian alternatives to the Yuppie career philosophy.

Tentmaking

Taking its name from the apostle Paul's occupation which supported his missionary endeavors, tentmaking emphasizes that career is a means rather than an end in itself. Working provides the financial support to allow the individual to carry on another ministry. Twenty hours of paid employment, for example, supports thirty hours of voluntary service, assisting an inner-city church in its ministry to deprived youngsters, helping out at a halfway house, or witnessing to high-school students through a group like Young Life.

Tentmaking also refers to short-term overseas projects whereby Christians can gain valuable cross-cultural experience, interacting with local believers while providing a developing country with expertise in teaching, building, finance, or health care.

Working at the Margins

Professional training and expertise can reap rich rewards in our society. Lawyers, doctors, financial analysts, and realtors are among those who, because of extensive training and demanding work, expect to gain a considerable degree of affluence as well as personal status. These expectations, affirmed by society at large, are challenged by biblical motifs of service and sacrifice. Rather than automatically entering the traditional career path, professionally trained Christians should consider using their gifts for those most in need. These are the members of our society who are frequently unable to take advantage of professional help and who have to make do with a lower standard of service. Christian lawyers might consider working in less plush surroundings in order to provide legal assistance for the poor. Doctors might respond to the needs of inner-city public hospitals, while those trained in areas related to housing may want to be concerned about low-cost accommodations for the urban poor as well as about high-rise apartments for the well-to-do. These examples can be multiplied many times to take in a wide variety of professions. Such commitment to the less fortunate members of society is not an easy route to take, but it displays a radical faithfulness to the biblical portrait of a loving God who is deeply concerned about those in need (Ps. 146).

Limited Lifestyle

A television commercial seductively urges us to "master the possibilities." A society run on credit encourages the accumulation of possessions and panders to the impulse to spend rather than save, to get rather than to give. The Christian response to the religion of materialism is halfhearted at best. Since the publication of Ronald Sider's book *Rich Christians in an Age of Hunger,* Christians have intermittently discussed the option of simple lifestyle, being appropriately shocked by Sider's analysis while largely failing to do anything about it. More recently, Sider's whole thesis has come under prolonged attack from those who see his criticism of Christian affluence as nothing but unwarranted "guilt-manipulation." "Simple lifestyle," an ambiguous and relative term, seems comfortably passé for many Christians—the world view of the urban professional can be endorsed with a clear conscience.

In the light of this dying debate, the Gospels make uncomfortable reading. A careful study of Luke's Gospel in particular reveals that Jesus repeatedly advocated an approach to living characterized by greater simplicity; he also forcefully opposed the accumulation of surplus wealth (Luke 12:15–21, 22–34; 9:3; 10:4). When we add to this Jesus' criticism of the rich (8:14; 16:19–31; 18:24–25; 21:1–4) and his praise for those who give up their possessions (18:26–30; 7:25; 19:8–10) it becomes clear that the challenge to adopt a limited lifestyle must be a permanent part of the Christian's agenda. The phrase *limited lifestyle* can be seen as parallel to the concept of limited growth at the macroeconomic level, suggesting the subordination of prosperity to such concerns as the protection of natural resources and the redistribution of wealth to the developing world. What the limits are for individual and family expenditures is a personal decision, albeit one preferably made in the context of a Christian fellowship that provides guidance and mutual support.

The emphasis that the gospel places upon what we have called limited lifestyle is clearly relevant for a discussion of Christian perspectives on work. First, it suggests that a high salary should be extremely low on the list of criteria for assessing career options. In fact, salary based upon need rather than upon entitlement should be given far more consideration within the Christian community than it presently receives. Second, considerable restraint should be shown in our expenditures, with the concept of limited lifestyle providing room for the legitimate enjoyment of the good things of God's creation coupled with an avoidance of superfluity.

Third, the balance between personal expenditure and giving to various aspects of the work of the kingdom should be tilted in favor of the latter.

What would Jesus have to say about the ethos of the modern marketplace? The profound description of our Lord in Philippians 2:5–8 can act as a powerful commentary on our contemporary culture. The apostle Paul writes:

> Your attitude should be the same as that of Christ Jesus:
> Who, being in very nature God,
> did not consider equality with God
> something to be grasped,
> but made himself nothing,
> taking the very nature of a servant,
> being made in human likeness.
> And being found in appearance as a man,
> he humbled himself and became obedient
> unto death—even death on a cross!

Our model is to be Christ and it is one not of upward mobility, but of downward humility.

Study Questions

1. What is the primary sense in which God calls us? How does this help us in placing the choice of a career in proper perspective?
2. What is the problem with the expression *full-time Christian service?* Do you agree with Martin E. Clark's statement that "secular careers are those in which one's living is earned by functions other than ministry"?
3. From your own experience and thinking how accurate are Clark's suggestions regarding the mechanics of a call? What additions, if any, would you make to these suggestions?
4. It has been said that tentmaking (in which a person takes a job simply in order to make enough to support himself in some form of Christian ministry) is the trend of the future. Discuss the advantages and disadvantages of this principle.
5. Brainstorm regarding "more challenging ways" in the following vocational areas: medicine, law, business, arts and media, education.
6. Do you think Christians are called to a simple lifestyle? If so, how are the limits of such a lifestyle determined?

Biblical Passages for Further Study

The following biblical texts are foundational to our understanding of the calling which we have as disciples of Jesus Christ. With the aid of different commentaries and study guides, examine the passages listed in order to deepen your understanding of God's Word and its applicability to this subject of calling:

1. God is the caller and we are the recipients of his call

   Matthew 4:18–22
   Matthew 9:9–13
   Matthew 22:1–3
   Romans 9:22–24
   Galatians 5:8
   1 Thessalonians 5:24

2. Biblical examples of a calling which involved a distinct (often audible) instruction from God regarding a specific task

   Exodus 3:1–10
   Amos 7:14–15
   Romans 1:1
   1 Corinthians 1:1
   Hebrews 5:4

3. To what are we called?

   a. Called to faith in Jesus Christ

      Romans 8:28–30
      1 Corinthians 1:9
      2 Thessalonians 2:13–15

   b. Called to the kingdom of God

      1 Thessalonians 2:10–12

   c. Called to eternal life

      1 Timothy 6:12
      Hebrews 9:15

   d. Called to holy living

      1 Corinthians 1:2
      1 Peter 1:15

   e. Called to specific church-related ministry

      Mark 3:13–19
      Acts 13:2–3
      Acts 16:6–10
      1 Corinthians 12:28

Additional suggestions for the serious Bible student:

1. Read 1 Corinthians 7:20 and Ephesians 4:1 in different translations of the New Testament, comparing contrasting versions such as the Revised Standard Version and the New International Version.
2. Study John Calvin's *commentary* on 1 Corinthians 7:20.

3. Analyze the issue further by studying Gerhard Kittel's *Theological Dictionary of the New Testament,* vol. 3, p. 489.
4. To be biblically accurate, how should we use the word *calling* and how do our career aspirations fit into this calling?

The Big Picture 4

Living Out Our Beliefs

If we go back to the basics—the biblical basics—we know that work is a God-ordained function which involves both blessing and curse. We know that God has given us a mandate to be stewards of his creation and to nurture it as his trustees and that we, in fact, are co-creators with God. To be truly human, according to God's design, is to be a creative, constructive person after God's own image.

As Christians we also know that as an act of God's grace we have been given the gift of eternal life and citizenship in his kingdom. As kingdom citizens, who desire to be faithful to their Lord, we are instructed to live holy and righteous lives and to be salt and light in the world. In short, we have been called by God and one aspect of that calling is our choice of jobs and careers.

In previous chapters we have seen how a biblical perspective helps us see that the issue of jobs and careers involves more than merely finding clever ways to assess our personal inventory of talents and interests. There are deeper things at stake. What are the motives that drive us in our pursuit of a career? Are we seeking righteousness in our quest for work? Do we seriously evaluate various types of work in terms of their real social consequences or cultural worth? Are we seeking to be salt and light in our labors?

We also need to realize ways in which our culture affects and molds our attitudes toward work. We need antibodies to protect us from the "you-can-have-it-all" message that is pounded into us on every side.

But even this is not enough. In discussing work it is imperative that we look beyond the individual. The personal aspect of the Christian faith is rooted in an individual's salvation by the grace of God through faith in Christ. Such personal salvation, however, leads not to the rugged individualism celebrated by contemporary North American society but to a recognition of personal responsibility for corporate and societal concerns. "My career," "my salary" and "my future" are illegitimate considerations if they are not part of a much larger concern for God's designs for human society. Be assured, God is deeply interested in our individual well-being; that is precisely why he warns us about making it our exclusive focus. Remember our calling: to love God, ourselves, and our neighbors as ourselves. We must continue in all three, even in career consideration. Discipleship involves living out our faith in the world in which God has placed us. This means that searching Scripture for guidance that speaks only to our personal behavior, motives, or interests (although important) misses much of our task. Rejoice—the Bible gives us the big picture and it provides principles that help us live out our beliefs in practical ways in the real world of work.

So What's Wrong?

Think for a moment about how our society views work and the marketplace. Whether it be television ads, popular songs, formal career-counseling programs, attitudes of corporate management or labor-union leaders, what are the general assumptions which lie below the surface in our culture? While we must quickly admit that these general assumptions are often unstated (in fact we might even be embarrassed to state them explicitly), they are a very real part of our environment and become powerful forces in shaping our values and our actions.

A brief summary of the general premises concerning work that permeate our society would include the idea that people are autonomous individuals who are by nature entitled to pursue their own interests. This belief, which is part of our European Enlightenment heritage, assumes that men and women will find fulfillment in self-determination. Freedom comes to mean "do your own thing." A related notion undergirding this conviction is that progress is understood as an ever-growing mastery over nature. Translated in practical terms, this means we do not have to apologize about our desire for more material goods and leisure time since that is what life is all about!

A second premise involves our general view of business corporations: corporations are legal entities in which growth in size and profit is the primary objective. Fierce competition between companies is assumed and legal constraints are there to curb excesses. The rules of survival mean that labor must be paid the lowest possible wage and products must to be sold for as high a price as the market will bear.

In a similar way, most people assume that the labor union is an expression of the collective self-interests of its members and that its primary task is to gain maximum benefits for those who carry the union card. As businesses push to make all they can for their owners and then, on a secondary level, their managers, labor unions serve as a counterforce for the workers.

All this results in a view of society which assumes an adversarial relationship between labor and management. The assumption is that society is made up of a collection of competing self-interests. We may admit that this is not what ought to be, but sadly it is what we must realistically accept as what is. Our ultimate hope, despite the overwhelming evidence, is that the desire for self-preservation will be strong enough to restrain our worst impulses and that self-interests will somehow result in an equilibrium. But must we accept all this to be realistic? Is this all there is?

We are experiencing many tensions and pains in our society and around the world today because the foregoing premises are biblically unsound and because society does not actually function very well on this kind of a basis. These, of course, are two sides of the same coin. God's Word is true because he is God and he said it; also, the world works better when it follows the instructions in the operating manual written by the One who holds the patent!

Society can not reach equilibrium by balancing tensions among competing self-interests. That's not God's intention for society or for civil authority. The fact is that the naked pursuit of self-interest is an erroneous basis for social organization because the natural tendency is for the more powerful to abuse their power at the expense of the weak and powerless. Labor unions, which single-mindedly pursue a goal of securing the largest piece of the economic pie for their members, will ignore the real problems of the marketplace (centered in the failure to view the worker as a responsible human being) because of the preoccupation with increased wages and benefits. Similarly corporation leaders should not possess all the rights of management simply because they supply the capital. To believe this obscures an accurate view of the corporation, which is above all else a working community. Similarly individualism, which elevates the pursuit of self-fulfillment and personal gratification above everything else, underestimates the destructive results of unleashed self-interest.

The Bible gives us the real picture. It not only gives the real picture for our personal lives, but also offers us a realistic vision of how society is designed to function. The biblical principles of justice and stewardship sketch God's design for how people relate to each other. Of course, we can be presumptuous. We can deny the Patent Holder's design. But we do so at our peril. People, created in God's image, were made to serve him and each other. Selfishness is destructive. It can never be a satisfactory basis for society.

Scripture repeatedly teaches us that we must avoid idolatry and that idolatry leads to injustice. Warnings in both the Old and New Testaments make this abundantly clear. The message of the prophets, for example, was that both tables of the law were important. God alone is to be worshiped and human relationships are to be regulated on the basis of justice. Israel failed on both counts. That should emphasize for us that the worship of false gods is linked to the rejection of justice. That pattern seems to be true throughout biblical history.

Although we do not worship images of Baal or participate in temple prostitution, these biblical insights can help us identify the idols in our own time, whether they are the idols of our popular culture or our own private gods. Our society's obsession with material abundance, the pursuit of pleasure and the avoidance of discomfort, the search for status and identity in our jobs—these are the idols of our day. These are the idols that lead us to the false premises that undergird our secular world view. And because they are idols they are powerful. They lead us to misunderstand our world and destructively affect us on both a personal and corporate level. They create an illusion that justifies our unjust acts—oftentimes because we neither think about our career search in these biblical terms nor examine Scripture to find what it says about these idols.

Neither Marx nor Markets

The solution to our present crisis cannot be found in the competing ideologies of our age. Karl Marx does not have the answer, nor do the advocates of contemporary free-market economics. Both of these ideologies are rooted in the same soil and both are wrong because they are built on false assumptions. Marx believed that when a pattern of creating wealth developed in a society, that society would divide into competing economic classes: wealth-owners (capitalists, which he called the bourgeoisie) and wealth-creators (workers, which he called the proletariat). History was a struggle of these competing economic classes, and Marx was convinced that the workers would ultimately triumph. Marx's belief in this outcome of history does not offer us any realistic hope for the future. As it has been implemented by his followers, Marxism has been shown to include tragic flaws. Marxist states are ideologically rigid and their citizens live under a repressive central political authority that claims, as the dictatorship of the proletariat, to be a people's democracy but actually works to protect the interests of its ruling elites. New forms of class division have replaced old ones.

The personal freedoms associated with open-market economies must not be taken lightly. We in the West have much for which to be thankful. But we Christians must be discerning. Although capitalism emerged in part because of the view of work expressed by leaders of the Reformation, contemporary free-market economic theory and practice are largely divorced from these early Reformation roots. What has emerged is an exaggerated individualism which argues that people and corporations are, and have a right to be, free to do what they want so long as their freedom does not restrict the ability of other people and corporations to exercise their freedom in a similar way. Translated into simple English, this means that my freedom to swing my arm ends at the beginning of your nose!

The Bible exposes the fallacies of both of these systems of

thought. Glorifying the state in a collectivist society and glorifying the individual in Western society are both idolatrous and will lead to injustice. The standard is not self-interest, whether for an economic class or for the individual, but justice. According to Scripture, justice is an attribute of God himself and he has given us instructions that we should live justly in society. For the Jews the biblical concept of justice was not an abstract idea but a relational one. Justice involves God relating to us and us to each other.

Although a lengthy discussion of biblical justice is not possible here, it is important to understand that justice involves, among other things, right relationships. Do we live in right relationship with each other? Interchange the words *justice* and *righteousness* as you read Scripture and you will begin to see more clearly what God intends for us in our social context. In every aspect of our lives—within our families, between families, between ethnic groups, between nations—God desires that we be rightly related. Not selfish, but in just relationship. We were created by God to glorify him and serve each other. We are called to glorify God in serving others and contributing to the common good.

What would happen if evangelical Christians began to recognize the idols of our time and started to unmask them? What if Christians in the United States refused to worship the idol of self-interest with its appetite for material abundance, the pursuit of pleasure and status? What if we articulated a vision for our society that is grounded in the principles of Scripture? What would that new vision look like?

A New Vision

The Bible offers us a sweeping critique of the idols of our day if we are willing to take God's Word seriously. And its message does not call for fine tuning but rather for a massive overhaul. Think for a moment about how biblical truths would drastically challenge our contemporary beliefs.

What if, instead of assuming an adversarial relationship between labor and management, we began with the premise that there should be harmony and cooperation? If Scripture is correct in revealing work as one way that men and women, regardless of their profession of faith, can serve God and each other and that our relationships in the workplace are to be just, we can commit ourselves to a vision of labor-management relations which is precisely contrary to the status quo. The general assumption that conflict exists between employer and employee should be exposed. We should not assume that this is normal, that this is the way it is and has to be. Rather than passively accepting this model, Christians should demonstrate by their actions, as well as by their testimonies, that there is in fact another option.

Some Christians in Canada have decided to take a radical stand on this issue and openly challenge the adversary system in the work world in their country. Founded in 1952, the Christian Labour Association of Canada (CLAC) has focused its attention on labor-management relations. One of its charter principles is the belief that "labour-management relations are, and ought to be, cooperative relationships, although the need to differentiate with respect to responsibility and authority must be acknowledged." These Christians are attempting to take the apostle Paul's teaching concerning reconciliation seriously. When Colossians 1 states that in Jesus Christ "all things hold together" both "in heaven and on earth" and that God has chosen to reconcile all things to himself through Jesus Christ (vv. 15–20), then this must be true. Instead of shrinking our understanding of reconciliation to a narrowly confined personal sphere, we should see this teaching in its fullness. Let us open our eyes to the whole truth of this message. Christ's reconciling work has implications for every aspect of our lives and Christ has called us to be reconcilers not only in the church and in our families, but in the marketplace as well.

We also need to challenge our contemporary view of the value of work and the worker. When the Roman Catholic bishops in the United States examined our economy in light of biblical revelation, they offered a "Christian vision of economic life" which was refreshing. They argued that "the dignity of the human person, realized in community with others, is the criterion against which all aspects of economic life must be measured." While we may disagree with some of the policy applications offered by the bishops in their pastoral letter, the sound biblical grounding for the statement about human dignity is clear.

Labor is not just a cost component, which we often describe in economic jargon as a disutility. Labor has value which goes beyond merely producing something; labor, as we described it earlier, is a cultural activity which involves our co-creational work as stewards of God's earth. A low view of labor leads to the creation of dehumanized work conditions, an environment where social contact between employees is severely reduced, and where technology can result in new forms of slavery.

A biblical view of work would suggest the need for enhancing our view of the laborer and might lead to a search for creative ways to encourage greater worker participation at various stages of the decision and production process. It would also suggest that laborers put less emphasis on rights and more emphasis on duties. It would change our present focus on workers' rights versus management's prerogatives to an emphasis on mutual tasks and mutual obligations.

Operating on this basis is not only biblically sound, but also realistic! Consider the case of Wayne Alderson. As vice president of operations at the Pittron Steel Foundry in Pittsburgh, Alderson implemented a vision for peace in the work world by developing a concept which he called "the value of the person." Using a leadership style based on the biblical principle of reconcilation, he worked to build love, dignity, and respect at Pittron. "Operation Turnaround" was successful: there was a 64 percent increase in production, an increased profit of twelve million dollars, and an improved work environment which virtually eliminated worker absenteeism.[1]

Another practical implication of a biblical view of work concerns employment policy. If all economic activity, according to Scripture, involves exercising our responsibility as God's stewards and is a fulfillment of our role as co-creators, and if our labor is the way we meet the material needs of ourselves, our families, and others in need, making a priority of finding jobs for people becomes critical in a nation's life. Unemployment not only causes deprivation with all its related social and economic costs, but also destroys a person's sense of importance and worth. We are not suggesting that it is the government's responsibility to guarantee everyone a job, but we are arguing that it must be a priority for all sectors of society to work for full employment if that society is to be a healthy one.

Scripture also focuses special attention on the needs of the poor. One of the principal characteristics of biblical justice is the

---

1. For the exciting story of Alderson's life and vision, read R. C. Sproul, *Stronger Than Steel: The Wayne Alderson Story* (New York: Harper and Row, 1983).

repeated emphasis on those people who are vulnerable and powerless. Repeatedly God identifies himself with the widow, the orphan, the foreigner, and the poor, reminding the Hebrews that they were once slaves in Egypt. The words of Deuteronomy 6 are a necessary reminder for all of us:

> When the LORD your God brings you into the land he swore to your fathers . . . to give you—a land with large, flourishing cities you did not build, houses filled with all kinds of good things you did not provide, wells you did not dig, and vineyards and olive groves you did not plant—then when you eat and are satisfied, be careful that you do not forget the LORD, who brought you out of Egypt, out of the land of slavery (vv. 10–12).

Making the needs of the poor a priority does not mean that Scripture supports the creation of a welfare state. The creation of increased dependencies can be the result of massive federal welfare programs. It does mean, however, that a priority for all sectors of society—our families, our churches, our businesses, and our government—ought to be increased economic participation by poor people. Their employment demands a proper share of our talent, energy, and wealth. Without it our society will not be a healthy one and our social fabric will increasingly be characterized by conditions of injustice.

The creative vision of John Perkins which he and his colleagues implemented through the Voice of Calvary Ministries in Mississippi is an exciting example for us. Perkins decided to follow Christ's teachings as they affected economic life. He built a series of community-level structures that have transformed the lives of many poor people. Voice of Calvary Ministries has grown to include housing and neighborhood rehabilitation, a thriftstore cooperative, youth recreation programs, a training/study center, a church, and a community health-education program.

John Perkins had a vision for people who have dignity because they are made in God's image and he prioritized the needs of those who lacked the opportunity to work their way out of poverty. Once again, Perkins's example demonstrates not only that biblical truths are morally right but also that society functions better when they are followed.[2]

2. For John Perkins's life story read his graphic autobiography, *Let Justice Roll Down* (Ventura, Calif.: Regal, 1976).

These implications of a biblically grounded vision of work in society are suggestive only in the broadest sense and need much refinement. Nor do they represent a complete list of possible implications. We have not addressed the issues of technology and what ought to guide its unfolding. Nor have we addressed the ways in which decisions in our country have an impact on the Third World; to act without regard for the harm caused by our decisions in a world of economic interdependence is to practice injustice. These are all complex issues that defy simple solutions, but Christians ought to be in the forefront of the debates addressing them.

Wrestling with the issues that affect the big picture is difficult, so if you are feeling overwhelmed your reaction is not unusual. If most of us have a vision for our lives, it usually does not extend much beyond our own limited surroundings. God's Word, however, puts our personal salvation story in the larger context of what God is doing in the world through history. We are called into his kingdom, which is made up of people from around the world, and we are instructed to be his agents in the world, empowered by his Holy Spirit.

No Excuses!

If we were honest with ourselves, most of us would have to confess that we live like atheists day to day. This does not mean that we openly sin and defy God's commandments, but that we operate under the assumption that God is as good as dead in certain areas of our lives. Do we really act as if we believe Jesus is Lord of our work and the marketplace? It is so easy to assume that our job requires certain kinds of behavior unconnected to the Word of God, which we restrict to the areas of our family or church life. It is convenient for us to live in different worlds, separate compartments governed by different rule-makers.

Oftentimes Christians limit discussion of their witness on the job to the subject of verbal expressions of their personal faith in Christ. Although this is an important dimension of Christian witness, it is not the whole story! Can you imagine what could happen if the hundreds of Christian businessmen's breakfast and luncheon groups would move beyond stories of personal conversions and techniques for sharing one's faith to serious discussion of how they might be agents of reconciliation in their offices, how the dignity of workers in their business could be enhanced, or how greater worker participation could be achieved in their companies?

Perhaps we have never been challenged to think in these terms. Maybe we feel too small to do anything about these big issues. Some of us probably feel that we will worry about these things *after* we establish ourselves in a profession. These are all excuses; we need to recognize that. Don't let the feeling "what can one person do?" be an obstacle for you. From a biblical perspective the issue of whether or not we will be successful if we follow God's commandments is not important. We are called to be faithful to God's Word and the rest is up to God. He has promised that if we abide in him we *will* bear fruit (John 15:5). We must stop trying to count fruit and focus on living a life of faithfulness. Our focus should be on faithfulness. After all, we know in the end there will be no excuses!

Study Questions

1. Do you agree with the thesis that Christians in our society often privatize or personalize their faith, thereby not considering the big picture very often? In your opinion, why has this happened?
2. Have you personally held to the general premises of our society (as summarized in this chapter) concerning individual autonomy and self-interest or the nature of corporations and labor unions? What other implicit assumptions would you add to this list?
3. How has contemporary capitalist thought and action divorced itself from governing norms that constrain its excesses?
4. How would you define idolatry? What are its characteristics?
5. How do biblical insights about idolatry help us see the idols of our time?
6. Who are the Christian heroes in your life? What models do you have of Christians who are committed to transforming work and the workplace for the glory of God?

Biblical Passages for Further Study

Serious biblical study of the subjects of idolatry and justice will help us understand the material discussed in this chapter. With the aid of different versions of the Bible, including those which paraphrase Scripture (J. B. Phillips) or use popular language (*Good News for Modern Man* or *The Living Bible*), study the passages that follow:

1. Prohibitions against idolatry

   Exodus 20:3–6
   Deuteronomy 7:25
   Deuteronomy 29:16–18
   Psalm 78:58

2. Israel's repeated practice of idolatry

   Exodus 32
   Judges 2:17
   Hosea 1:2

3. Idolatry means worshiping something people, rather than the Creator, made

   Psalm 115:4–8
   Isaiah 2:8
   Isaiah 40:18–20
   Romans 1:23
   1 Corinthians 8:4

4. People, by nature, are religious and are inclined to worship false gods

   Galatians 5:20
   1 Thessalonians 1:9

5. New Testament warnings against idolatry

   1 Corinthians 10:6–14
   1 John 5:21
   Colossians 3:5

6. People become like the idols they worship

    Psalm 115:8
    Jeremiah 2:5
    Hosea 9:10

7. God is a God of justice

    Deuteronomy 32:4
    Psalm 35:10
    Psalm 146:5–9

8. Old Testament regulations concerning a just economy

    Leviticus 19:9–10
    Leviticus 25

9. New Testament insights on economic justice

    Acts 2:42–47
    Acts 4:32–35
    Ephesians 4:28
    2 Thessalonians 3:6–10

10. "Being holy" and "doing justice"

    Micah 6:6–8
    Isaiah 58

5 On the Job: Christians Talk About Their Work

In 1974 Studs Terkel wrote a significant and controversial book entitled *Working: People Talk About What They Do All Day and How They Feel About What They Do.* The book consists of numerous interviews with people from many different walks of life. These people offer bluntly honest assessments of their working lives. Terkel is particularly concerned to draw out the bleaker aspects of employment—the drudgery, frustration, mistreatment of workers, and the sheer burden of labor.

The interviews that follow might be seen as a brief Christian response to Terkel's sociological pessimism. Christians should have a distinctive view of the nature of work that is formed from an understanding of biblical principles. Such a perspective needs to be at least as honest as Terkel's treatment but can provide a more positive vision of working life based upon the principles outlined in previous chapters—co-creativity and calling, service and stewardship.

If Terkel's book was a brilliant exposé of the fallen nature of work, then the purpose of the following interviews is to illustrate that in Christ, both work and worker can be redeemed.

Stewardship: Managing in Christ's Name

Dennis Bakke

After graduating from Harvard Business School, Dennis Bakke worked at the Department of Health, Education and Welfare and then at the White House on energy-conservation programs. He did further study in international relations at the National War College and followed that with a spell as Deputy Director of the Energy Productivity Center. In 1981 he helped to found Applied Energy Services (AES), an unregulated utility producer of steam and electricity. He is currently executive vice president of AES. Dennis is married; he and his wife are active in the Washington Community Fellowship Church.

Q. Since you founded Applied Energy Services in 1981, the work force has grown from 6 to 180 and sales have risen by a similar extent. Would you say that such prosperity is a sign of God's blessing on your venture?

A. We have to be careful when using the term *blessing* to describe financial success and material prosperity. The blessing is not so much the abundance brought about by the growth of the company but the extra responsibility in terms of the stewardship of increased resources. In a sense, blessing and burden are mixed in that "to whom much has been given, much is expected." The key is greater responsibility rather than greater prosperity for its own sake.

Q. Could you describe some of the ways in which your management style is influenced by your Christian faith?

A. I can identify five main factors. First, every good manager is a decision-maker, a risk-taker. If your identity is tied up with the success of the business, you will inevitably be afraid of failure, restricting your ability to make bold decisions. A Christian manager has the freedom to make those decisions because the central focus is on Christ. Your identity comes from your relationship with Christ and there is no need to be hung up about business failure.

Second, managers are problem-solvers. Their task is to clear away obstacles in order to enable other members of the company to use their gifts to the full. Essentially, the manager performs the role of servant, as opposed to the popular conception of the boss. The manager facilitates the work of others, promoting their efficiency and abilities, giving them the credit whenever possible.

65

Christian managers should be particularly willing to demonstrate qualities of servanthood.

Third, a major part of the manager's job is teaching, and Christians have the ultimate example in the person of Jesus. The effectiveness of his teaching of the disciples had a lot to do with the fact that he spent so much time with them, getting to know their weaknesses and their strengths. In the same way, managers need to know their staff, need to be available to them when they have problems and questions.

Fourth, stamina and health are crucial factors in a manager's success. As Christians we believe that our bodies are important and ought to be looked after as part of our stewardship.

Fifth, and perhaps most important, is the issue of motivation. Christian managers should not be working for power, status, and wealth but as a service to Jesus Christ. While worldly objectives can be fairly compelling, Christian commitment can provide a sense of mission and purpose that is even more powerful and certainly more enduring. If we really believe we are working "as to the Lord," we will be dedicated and enthusiastic managers.

Q. The position of executive vice president must provide the temptation to become so committed to the job that it becomes an idol. How have you avoided the extreme of workaholism?

A. The difference between doing God's will in the workplace and turning work into an idol is so small that you have to check yourself almost every day. We need to be in the Scriptures regularly and to have people to whom we are accountable. We need to be part of a church fellowship that calls us back to a focus on Jesus Christ.

Q. Your salary is presumably higher than those of most other Christians in your local church. How do you handle that inequality and how do you go about the allocation of your income?

A. When we founded the company and saw it begin to grow, my wife and I realized that we might be faced with a major stewardship responsibility. It became clear that it would be possible for us to dominate the financial giving of the local fellowship and we realized that would be harmful. We sought counsel from other believers and have a policy of discussing our family budget with our small covenant group. For us the biblical principle of stewardship means that everything we possess belongs to the Lord. Our home, for example, is his, and should be used as a means of furthering his kingdom. As far as financial giving is concerned, we decided to set up a foundation with our two families making up the board of directors. In this way we are able to decide together how to allocate grants to various Christian activities.

Company profit needs to be distributed with the same concern for stewardship. We have therefore set up a program by which the company will match one for one every dollar given by employees to a tax-exempt charitable organization, including churches.

Q. With regard to the employment policy of the company, should a Christian employer practice positive discrimination, selecting disadvantaged people and minorities?

A. For me the key to employment policy is looking for people who will be able to use their gifts effectively. It is a disservice to place people in jobs for which they don't have the required talents. On the other hand, we must avoid selecting only the type of people with which we're familiar—white, middle class, for example. My own background is not a privileged one and I am somewhat predisposed to give opportunities to those from humble backgrounds. If there is a significant risk that a person won't be able to do the job, however, we would not think it appropriate to practice reverse discrimination. There is no biblical warrant for producing less than the best, although the product must never become more important than people.

Q. Imagine you're talking to a Christian young person who has recently graduated from college and expresses a desire to become a corporate executive. What advice would you give to that person at the outset of his career?

A. I would focus on the issue of motivation. I would want to probe why he has the desire to be a corporate executive. Is it a longing to be rich, powerful, and respected or a desire to use God-given managerial skills to the full? If the motivation is Christ-centered I would stress that biblical principles are undoubtedly the best tools for effective management enabling a Christian manager to be a faithful steward of God's resources.

Working Women, Ambition, and Knowing When to Quit
Debbie Price

Debbie Price obtained a bachelor of science degree in interior design and was head interior designer for a company in Aspen,

Colorado, for five years. A significant career change took place when Debbie joined the staff of a Baptist church as administrative assistant and education director. During this seven-year period she was also on the associate staff of Young Life. Debbie then moved to Washington, D.C., to manage the office of the National Prayer Breakfast and also to work at the Fellowship Foundation. For the last two years Debbie has been personal secretary in charge of scheduling for Senator William Armstrong from Colorado. Out of office hours, Debbie helps to lead a large singles group at Fourth Presbyterian Church in Bethesda, Maryland.

Q. Debbie, you have worked in a variety of positions, including church-based jobs, being on the staff of a parachurch organization, and in several so-called secular positions. Would you say that the church-related positions were more pleasing to God than the others—that so-called full-time Christian work is more honoring to him?

A. I don't think God prefers one over the other. The issue God looks at, I believe, is not what you do but how and why you do it— what your motivations are.

Q. What are your motivations for working?

A. At the risk of sounding pious, I have to say that the primary motivation is a desire to glorify God in my job by using the gifts he has given me. A second motivation is the development of my faculties—mental, spiritual, and physical—through the tasks of work.

Q. Are you ambitious?

A. Not particularly. At least not in the world's understanding of that term. I do think God wants us to be the best we can be and holds us accountable for the use we make of our gifts. We should therefore endeavor to do our work as well as possible. It's good that some Christians are given the motivation to strive to become chairman of the board, but a person in a lower position is no less important to God nor any less ambitious if he is desiring to serve the Lord. Ambition, as the world understands it, has the danger of blurring the focus of why we work. The competitive drive can take over and you can neglect the question of where God wants you to be. When I interviewed with Senator William Armstrong for my present position, he said he would give me time to look around for other possibilities before committing myself. I was able to accept his offer immediately, however, because I didn't feel the need to hunt down the very "best" job I could find. It was far more important to me to get the job that I felt called to be doing.

Q. Your mention of feeling called raises an important point. Do you believe that God has one job that he intends for you? Are you now meant to be in the Senator's office and nowhere else?

A. I believe that God has given us free will to choose courses of action but that he does guide us—that is the permanent tension in a Christian understanding of decision making. The fact that God has given each of us certain gifts narrows down the range of career options. You can tell when you're in a job that you're meant to be in, but there may be several that fit into that category.

Q. Could you describe some of the criteria for determining the kind of work in which a person should be?

A. First, it's very important to understand where your strengths and weaknesses lie. A group of Christians can really help one another in this regard. The kind of honesty required can be painful at times but it's very helpful in the long run. Second, you should consider what the job is asking you to do. The product of your work is most important. Is the result of your labor truly worthwhile, serving the community and honoring God? The worth of the job in God's eyes can become clear as we pray about a specific job option.

Q. What is your attitude to witnessing to colleagues at work? How can you communicate your faith in a sensitive way?

A. First of all, witnessing is not an option, but a command. I think of "witness" not as a verb but as who you are. I'm a witness whether I'm a good witness or not. As far as how we witness is concerned, Becky Pippert has a great expression: "We're called to be fishers of men, not hunters of men." This involves answering questions as they're asked and expressing your faith in natural ways. For me evangelism is primarily relational—we have to win the right to be heard by showing our concern for the other person's needs.

Q. Do you think that a Christian woman should have the same view of work as a Christian man?

A. No. Although there's certainly nothing wrong with women working and combining that with family life, I think a woman will frequently view career and finances differently from a man. It is much less likely that a woman will be the sole provider for a family and men are therefore more conscious of the responsibility of being the breadwinner. That does not affect the value of the work done, however. A woman's work is identical in value to that of a man and opportunities should also be identical.

Q. You are a professional woman working in an influential position—you ration access to a Senator of the United States. On the other hand, you could say, "I'm just a secretary." What would you say to the person who says, "I'm just a secretary," and then what would you say to someone who continually brings up the fact that he works for a Senator of the United States?

A. I think both have an unhealthy attitude. You should not take a job so seriously that prestige is a big factor. True respect is a product of who you are, not what you do. A desire for prestige has the danger of making you believe things about yourself that aren't true—that you're more valuable than someone else. On the other hand, more menial or subordinate positions are no less prestigious in God's eyes.

Q. I believe there was a time when you became unhappy in your work. How did you decide that leaving the job would be better than pressing on in the hope that it would improve?

A. It was a hard decision. I finally made it when I realized I wasn't being valuable to anyone. Nor was I able to be enthusiastic about any aspect of my work. I also realized that it wasn't right for me to be doing what the job required. Not that there was anything dishonest or illegal involved, but I was being paid on a commission basis—30 percent of the gross profit. One client spent twenty thousand dollars on furnishings for a 10 x 12 room. I began to question my motivation for encouraging people to buy—I really couldn't believe that it was good stewardship of my talents to be persuading customers to spend huge sums of money on furniture. So, although it was a lucrative position, I decided to leave. If you're in doubt about the value of your job, ask yourself two questions: Am I being faithful? And am I being fruitful? They are the key terms for me.

Witnessing by "Doing Justice"
Herbert Barksdale

Herbert Barksdale is a solid-looking man whose large hands provide evidence that he was once a professional boxer. As a black growing up in the context of segregation, Herbert developed a passion for justice and racial harmony. When he became a Christian as a young man, he determined to integrate his new faith with all aspects of his life, including the workplace and civil-rights issues. Herbert is particularly interested in labor-management relations and spends much of his time facilitating dialogue between representatives of the two sides of industry. Since 1979 Herbert has been an investigator for the Office of Paternity and Child Support Enforcement in Washington, D.C.

Q. Herbert, I believe you've had a varied working life. Tell us about some of the jobs you've had.

A. When I was seventeen I became a professional boxer and did that for four years. I guess I won some and I lost some! After that I ran a numbers game in a black area of Washington. It was something like a state lottery on a much smaller scale. Occasionally I would do really well and make quite a bit of money. It was during this time that I began to get interested in racial issues as I encountered the reality of prejudice in segregated Washington.

During the Korean War I was in the Navy and was involved in some of the fighting. I enjoyed the image of being the tough guy. After the war I drove a taxicab for eight years and just about met the whole world driving around Washington.

Q. Were you a Christian at this time?

A. No, but it was through some of the conversations I had in the cab that I began to be aware of what commitment to Jesus Christ meant, and in 1968 I made that commitment.

Q. How did that affect your attitude to your work?

A. To begin with, I thought that now I was a Christian I had to get a "Christian" job where I'd be doing "full-time ministry." So I became a counselor at a Methodist church and did that for two years. Now that was good work, but I began to realize that you don't have to work in a church if you're a Christian. God wants people in all kinds of positions and you can serve him in the business world, in government, in education or wherever.

Q. Does that include politics?

A. Certainly it does. Relating Christian faith to public policy issues is one very important way in which we can serve our Lord. I believed I was doing that in 1974 when I was the director of the distribution of materials for a mayoral campaign here in D.C. Not that God's on the side of any particular party, but I think he does want us to think and act as Christians in the political arena.

Q. What are you doing now?

A. Since 1979 I've been working as an investigator for the Office of Paternity and Child Support Enforcement in Washington, D.C. It's demanding work, but I get a lot of satisfaction out of helping some of the most needy members of our society.

Q. I believe you have a particular interest in labor relations.

A. It's one of the most important issues as far as I'm concerned and one in which the Christian faith is very relevant. The New Testament advocates harmonious working relationships on the basis of respect and fair treatment. And yet in our society we see injustices being done to workers, subtle forms of racism, and generally a lack of cooperation.

Q. How have you been involved?

A. I'm part of an interesting prayer group that meets twice a month. The group includes the mayor of Washington, D.C., and the heads of government departments and seeks to bring harmony and spirituality to the workplace through dialogue between workers and management. What better way to dialogue than by praying together? I'm trying to widen the range of this because I believe there are many Christians out there at many different levels who don't know how to relate their faith to their work. Improving industrial relations by means of prayer groups is one of the best ways.

Q. Do you find it easy to witness to your faith at work?

A. My relationship with Jesus Christ is the most important thing to me and I find that I just have to talk about it with colleagues at work. It's important to do so in a loving manner that respects the other person's individuality and opinions. You also have to make sure that the way you work and your behavior generally support rather than contradict your verbal witness.

To me witnessing also involves standing up for justice in the workplace, challenging abuses in the treatment of employees, unethical practices, or anything that clearly goes against the will of God. When people know that your faith is what motivates you to take a stand, even to the point of challenging the boss, it's a powerful witness to Christ.

Guidance, Goal-Setting, and Government Responsibility
Mel Loewen

From truck-driving on the Canadian prairies to founding and running a university in Africa, Mel Loewen has had a fascinating and varied working life. Reared in a Mennonite family in an underdeveloped part of Canada, Mel was encouraged by his parents to seek out opportunities to further his education. He earned a doctoral degree from the University of Brussels and went with his wife to the Belgian Congo (now Zaire) to be a teacher under the auspices of a Christian organization. Mel directed a teacher-training school in an isolated bush area and was a member of the National Commission on Higher Education. He was later decorated by the president for helping to found a university in the newly independent Zaire. After more than ten years in Africa, the Loewen family returned to the United States, where Mel became the academic dean of a college and a consultant for the World Bank. Since 1973 Mel has been an educational adviser for the Bank (based in Washington, D.C.), and in August 1986 took up an ambassador-level position as the Bank's representative in Rwanda, Central Africa.

Q. I get the impression that you enjoy your work?

A. Yes, for me work is an essentially positive and productive cause. I pity the person who wins one million dollars in the lottery and has the fun of spending it but not the joy of making it. The converse is also true—one feels sorry for the person who labors in a productive manner but never receives the due reward.

Q. You have experienced a number of career changes. What is your understanding of guidance in such a process?

A. Many schemes have been developed to demonstrate how guidance works. Some have seven points, others seventeen, but I find that three are sufficient. First, we should look at the general revelation of Scripture, for it provides a broad picture of the sort of life that is honoring to God. That picture is the necessary context in which to make career decisions. Second, what are the particular needs of this generation at this time—what are the pressing concerns of the day? Having assessed where the needs lie, determine how your natural capacities might be developed in order to meet those needs. Third, be open to what the Holy Spirit may be saying to you. This may take the form of the opening and closing of doors as you apply for various positions. Sometimes the Spirit may prompt you to defy all logic and try something completely different, although it should be said that this is the exception rather than the rule.

Q. Do you think a special sense of calling is required for overseas missionary service or for the full-time pastorate?

A. When my wife and I decided to go to Zaire as educators with a Christian organization, it seemed the obvious extension of a commitment to the developing world that had been fostered during childhood and years of training. I can't say we had a particularly dramatic sense of calling, although, as God works in many different ways, other believers may well experience a clear demonstration of the Holy Spirit's leading.

Q. Do you think the distinction between full-time Christian service and secular work is a useful one?

A. I think I know less about what full-time service means now than I did when I was a young man. The person who works in a factory and sends in a regular contribution to support the one involved in missionary work—is he any less involved in full-time service than the one whom he helps to send? In the world of work, it is essential that Christians remember that they are all parts of the body of Christ and there is no place for saying that the mouth is superior to the feet.

Q. Goal-setting has become a much-used term in Christian circles recently. What role has goal-setting played in your own career development?

A. I have always set for myself the general goal of meeting tough challenges, of taking difficult assignments, because I think Christians should be people who are prepared to take on a lot of work. At the same time, I have found it useful to set for myself intermediate checkpoints after taking up a particular post in order to ascertain if I was handling the responsibilities and obtaining sufficient results to vindicate my having that position instead of somebody else. I have seen some people overreaching themselves and being devastated by failure. Periodic assessment of one's own work can prevent that, as it can the other extreme, which is floating through life in a job that doesn't require that you utilize your talents to the full.

Q. The various positions you have held have required that you and your family be mobile and prepared to live in many different contexts. Has that entailed a loss of security and identity on the part of your children?

A. Certainly my children don't have the roots that my wife and I had. Sometimes it hasn't been quite clear where home is. That is one of the sacrifices that Christians have to make if they believe God desires them to serve overseas for periods of time. I think I would advise a young couple faced with this possibility to establish a home base before going overseas so that the children have a sense of belonging. Ideally that home base should be maintained even during the time spent overseas.

Q. You emphasized earlier that work is God's intention for human beings. High unemployment figures in many countries mean that many people do not have the opportunity to fulfill this aspect of God's calling. Do you think, therefore, that it is the government's responsibility to provide work for all?

A. It is terribly sad to see people out of work, particularly young people. While I believe that everybody who is able should be employed, I feel that the government's role should be that of employer of last resort. Nobody owes me a job and Christians shouldn't be looking to government to provide them with employment. The Christian student who is graduating should not ask the question "Who will give me a job?" but "How can I create a job?" At the national level, of course, there needs to be a safety net, and government should offer jobs on social-welfare projects. Perhaps a more positive Christian response to the problem of unemployment would be for individuals to develop a variety of skills in order to ensure greater adaptability in the marketplace. The same could be said of those in church-related or missionary positions. Overspecialization should be avoided and I think we will see an increasing need for tentmakers—Christians with flexible working abilities, by which they can serve a developing country while simultaneously witnessing to the faith in Christ that motivates such service.

Respect and Responsibility: Key Themes for a Working Couple
Bob and Carol Hamrin

Career—family; ambition—parenting; professional status—parenthood. Where do they all fit for the Christian?

Bob and Carol Hamrin, the parents of three young children, have given considerable thought to the issues facing a working Christian couple. They both hold doctoral degrees, Carol in Chinese history and Bob in economics. Since 1975 Carol has been a political analyst for the Department of State. Bob began his career as an assistant professor of economics before moving to Washington, D.C., to work for the Joint Economic Committee of

Congress. He has also worked as economic adviser to Senator Gary Hart, and has spent the last three years consulting and writing. Carol and Bob are great believers in joint ministry and, early in their married life, shared a part-time position as a church youth pastor. For the last several years, they have been active in The C. S. Lewis Institute for Lay Biblical Studies in Washington, D.C.

Q. Bob and Carol, you both hold professional positions which obviously take a lot of your time. You also have three young children. Some people might feel that you are being somewhat irresponsible in continuing both of your careers when your first priority should really be your family. How would you respond to such criticism?

A. (Carol) At the heart of our approach to this issue has been the belief that Christians should use and develop their God-given talents. My career has enabled me to do that. Before we had children we committed ourselves to fully sharing the responsibilities of parenting. When we had our first child, I took three months off and then returned to full-time work. We both arranged flexible hours so as to keep the time Eric, our son, spent with a sitter to a minimum. Three years later when, to our great surprise, we produced twins, it was obvious that it was going to be considerably more difficult to combine career with a family. I remember Bob asking me why I wouldn't just quit working like other women did in order to look after the family. My response was that there wasn't any reason why I shouldn't consider that possibility but there wasn't any reason he shouldn't consider doing the same. We resolved that we would both make sacrifices in order to spend a good amount of time with our children. I took a two-day-a-week job with the Foreign Broadcast Information Service, and Bob arranged to spend one day a week at home.

When the twins were two, however, I decided to return full-time to the State Department; but that soon became very difficult. I was under considerable pressure at work and wasn't able to devote enough attention to my family. After a long struggle, praying and discussing the issue with friends, I came to a point where I could hand in a letter of resignation. God showed me that I had too much of my identity wrapped up in my career and that I needed to be able to give it all up if need be. I believe God honored that decision, because the State Department managed to create a part-time position for me and more recently gave me a twenty-month sabbatical in order to write a book on China's current reforms.

Q. Bob, how have biblical principles guided the way you have sought to combine career and family?

A. (Bob) The basic biblical principle in this area for me is that we are to respect our spouse. That includes helping them foster the gifts that God has given them. My respect for Carol in the career field has allowed me to make the trade-offs that have facilitated the development of her career as well as mine. I was prepared to spend a year in Hong Kong to allow Carol to work on her Ph.D. and then she was willing to come to Idaho for a year so that I could take up a teaching appointment.

Another principle is that of parental commitment. I decided that I wanted to play a significant role in the lives of my children from their earliest years on. I've had two marvelous opportunities to do that—first, when I left the Joint Economic Committee of Congress for nine months to work on a book at home, and for three months in 1979 in China when Carol worked in the embassy. During both periods, I was permanently at home with the children and thoroughly enjoyed it.

Q. Have you had to make sacrifices in ambition in order to keep the family at the center of your focus?

A. (Carol) In the last five years, both of us have made career decisions that have taken us off the ladder of success. I have watched my colleagues moving up the scale past me while I worked on a part-time basis. But the process of prayerfully dealing with that has been extremely beneficial in that it has led me to re-evaluate the meaning of success. When we came out of graduate school we thought that we would really have an impact on the world through our careers and would be successful in that sense. We have realized increasingly, however, that what God wants is to reshape and remake each one of us to become more like Christ. Our responsibility as husband and wife and as parents is primarily to help each other in that process.

Christians should assume from the outset that they will have to forfeit much of what the world counts as success. The world's understanding of success is often at the expense of other values and relationships which are central to our faith commitment. What you find, however, is that it doesn't turn out to be a sacrifice at all because God has an incredible way of providing blessings which more than compensate. This was demonstrated to me in

November 1985 when I was in China for research interviews. Fifteen years earlier I had written my doctoral dissertation on a Chinese Marxist-Leninist theoretician and director of the Communist Party school for top leaders. Last November, I was able to meet this man, was the first American to visit the Central Party School, and had the privilege of sharing my faith with him and other top school officials. It's clear to me that only God could have brought that about. Since we became willing to sacrifice career success, we have been much more conscious of God's direct leading of those careers.

A. (Bob) Christians should beware of the world's promise that they "can have it all." We have realized that our proper responsibility as parents requires that both of us scale back our ambitions. In 1983 I was working for Senator Gary Hart. When he announced that he was joining the presidential race, I was told that I should be prepared to stay at work until nine o'clock in the evenings as well as working on weekends. I decided that while my children were between the crucial ages of two and ten I should spend as much time with them as possible. So I resigned from the Hart campaign and launched off on my own. For the last three years I have been doing consulting projects and writing a couple of books. Next year, as I work on another writing project, I will continue to spend three days a week at home. Certainly we have experienced a cutback in income and I have had to give up the idea of being a prestigious academic economist or going to the top in the field of government. But I have never been more stretched spiritually than I have in the last three years. I have regained a sense of dependency on God that can so easily be lost as a result of professional status and substantial income. Of course our careers will remain important to us and will be the source of much satisfaction, but they are now in their proper place, subordinate to our commitment to the Lord, to each other, and to the nurturing of our three children.

Study Questions

1. Do you agree with Dennis Bakke's view of the limited role of reverse discrimination in employment policy?
2. As you read the interview with Herbert Barksdale, can you think of other specific ways of witnessing by doing justice?

3. Debbie Price suggests that a Christian woman is likely to have a different view of work from a man. Do you agree?
4. Mel Loewen feels that the government's role in providing jobs for the unemployed is only that of employer of last resort. Discuss the advantages and disadvantages of this as opposed to a more active governmental role of extensive job-creation programs.
5. What are the key elements in Bob and Carol Hamrin's success in combining professional lives with family responsibilities?

6 Now What?

Beware of the Traps

As we think about the subject of our jobs and future career aspirations, we need to pause a moment in order to thank God for his graciousness to us. God has not left us on our own to struggle in the darkness, groping to find direction for our lives where there are no discernible landmarks. All Scripture is "God-breathed" and is "useful," so each one of us may be "thoroughly equipped for every good work" (2 Tim. 3:16–17). That is an exciting truth. Despite the difficulties of the issues we face as we try to assess our own gifts and abilities and how we should use them in our work, we have a priceless resource available to us.

Scripture has both a positive and negative function. It gives us guiding principles for living, but it also warns us what to avoid as it unmasks our idols and knocks over their altars. The Bible's warning, of course, can be painful. No one enjoys having his idols stripped naked and toppled. But if we are to live in the light of biblical principles we must first suffer the pain of having our idols exposed. Bringing our idols into the open exposes our deepest commitments and when the objects of these commitments are shown to be of no value, that hurts. But no pain, no gain—so what have we been warned about?

We must be discerning about how our deepest faith convictions have been molded by our surrounding culture. How many times have we been reminded of the apostle Paul's warning: "Do not conform any longer to the pattern of this world" (Rom. 12:2)? Did you ever notice that Paul's words assume the believers in Rome *would* conform to the world? Warning about idolatry is a major theme in Scripture because the Lord knows we "got to worship somebody." We are created as religious beings and we will worship the true God or some other gods.

Baptizing the Yuppie mentality with a Christian vocabulary is one form of our cultural conformity. The logic is strikingly simple: God calls us to excellence; we must commit ourselves to exceptional performance in our jobs, even if it means sacrifice, and we will be blessed by all the benefits of career advancement. What we have done, of course, is empty these words (excellence, sacrifice, and blessing) of their biblical content and pour in the world's meaning. Just think for a moment. What do the Scriptures say is the type of excellence God expects from us who believe? What kind of sacrifice are we expected to make and for what reason? What constitutes a blessing in the Bible, and on whose act does it depend?

Another way we allow our culture to break down our biblical defenses is by thinking and living in two different worlds. Earlier we called this Christian dualism. Our faith is private and personal and may in fact be evidenced by vital devotional times each day, but the rest of our lives—our jobs, our income tax, our driving—is separate and has different types of rules governing behavior in these areas. The tragic result of this is that we wind up accepting the status quo because we do not really believe it can be changed. We resonate to the television news commentator's words, "That's the way it is. . . ." Although we might hesitate to admit it, many of us believe that God's instructions for kingdom living are helpful for our private lives, and perhaps our church lives, but certainly not for the marketplace.

This Christian dualism can also be seen by the way in which we attempt to worship both God and mammon, despite the Bible's clear teaching that this cannot be done (Matt. 6:24). Why does it take us so long to realize that the pursuit of wealth is a waste of our lives? King Solomon said it so clearly: "Whoever loves money never has money enough; whoever loves wealth is never satisfied with his income. This too is meaningless" (Eccles. 5:10). *The Liv-*

ing Bible puts this text in even more graphic words: "He who loves money shall never have enough. The foolishness of thinking that wealth brings happiness!" The deepest longings of our hearts can never be satisfied by money or prestige or worldly acclaim. We may agree with these words, but our lives show that we do not really believe them.

For many of us, our idolatry is not so obvious. We are not so crass that we are blindly going after the "big dollar." Instead our idolatry takes a much more subtle form. We fall into another trap: we believe that a successful job can be the context for the faithful Christian life rather than the faithful Christian life serving as the context for a successful job. This is a subtle distinction, but like most distinctions, it is important. It means that on a practical level we consider the search for a successful job as the given and, once it has been found, we *then* ask how can we work in our job as a Christian.

This distortion of truth confuses us. When we are convinced that our happiness, success, or fulfillment as a person will come from finding a "fulfilling" job, we relegate our faith to "Christian values" that we apply to our work behavior (keeping us honest, dependable, hard-working). But this is all backwards. Instead of finding happiness by being a slave to Christ, we become enslaved to things that make us happy.

In addition to the ways that our culture molds our value system and dictates our faith (ways that are sometimes exceedingly subtle and sometimes not!), there are other traps that are especially dangerous for Christians. These traps result from a confused understanding of biblical truth. The problem here is our wrong understanding about what our calling is and the related problem of confusing our vocation with our job. The problem is ours, and it cannot be blamed on some ambiguity or contradiction in Scripture.

The New Testament never uses the word which we translate "vocation" to mean an occupation or type of employment. The word is always used in a spiritual sense, in terms of our special calling to be children of God, to be citizens of God's kingdom. The apostle Paul establishes this powerfully in the well-known passage found in Romans 8: "And we know that in all things God works for the good of those who love him, who have been called according to his purpose. For those God foreknew he also predestined to be conformed to the likeness of his Son . . ."

(vv. 28–29a). We have been called as disciples of Jesus Christ to be Christ-like. Our central meaning and identity are wrapped up in our relationship with Jesus. Only in a derived sense can we biblically talk about our jobs as a calling.

Our employment is only a part of our larger calling in the same way that our worship and leisure activities are. If we belong to Christ, we must serve him in every area of our lives, including our work, our worship, and our recreation. The central issue is this: our jobs are *not* our vocation. We need to avoid that trap. Our vocation—to be conformed to the likeness of Christ—is much more significant and glorious than our jobs!

This biblical distinction is important because, without recognizing it, we can get ourselves trapped in numerous ways. One obvious danger is the way Christians describe their job search in terms of seeking their calling, when what they are really doing is developing a defense against anxiety. Using words like "I have been called into politics or law" can be a defensive ploy. It protects one from threatening self-examination or the consequences of having made the wrong choice. If someone says he was called by God into a certain career, there is not much room for discussion! There is no personal choice (because God told me!) and no anxiety (what else could I do!).

Another result of a confused understanding of calling is the implication that God has a plan for our lives, which we sometimes interpret to mean he has only one right choice for our careers. This can result in great anxiety (will I find the *right* career, the one God has chosen just for me!) or irresponsibility (I am waiting for God to find me a job!). In the latter case, career decision-making is seen as God's responsibility, not ours. We therefore make excuses for not assessing our own abilities and interests. The process of choosing a career then becomes mysterious and irrational and we wind up full of anxiety and doubt because our basis for choosing a job is grounded on nothing but vague internal feelings.

Scripture tells us that we are called to be disciples of Jesus Christ and that faith in him requires that we remove all other gods and worship him alone in every aspect of our lives. *That* is God's desire for us. Why not preserve the word *calling* for that usage and avoid the trap of narrowing down its meaning to apply to our job! We will only properly understand a biblical perspective on work when we get that straight.

Principles to Guide Us

So much for the nos and don'ts of Scripture. We have been warned about avoiding cultural conformity and instructed to be discerning about subtle forms of idolatry. The Bible does more than just give us warnings, however; it also helps us understand what God's desire is for our lives and what God is doing in history. It offers us principles that serve as guidelines for the decisions we must make. It is not a blueprint for our lives (that would lead to a boring existence just following the instructions from dot one to dot two to . . .), but it provides a foundation and a perspective so we can be faithful disciples in today's world.

First, we need a clear understanding of our calling as disciples of Jesus Christ, a call to faith offered to us by God's grace without any merit on our part. It is a call to citizenship in the kingdom of God; it is a call to live under Christ's lordship. God does the calling. And his call has significance for every aspect of our lives. As we realize that God's calling is not to a job, we need to deepen our understanding of what our calling really does mean. We have been called into a special relationship with God and, once we profess faith in him and repent of our old ways, we are on the path to becoming "new creations" (2 Cor. 5:17).

The implication of this truth is a profound one: we must make the goal of getting to know God more deeply the top priority in our lives. The prophet Jeremiah tells us not to boast of our wealth, our physical strength, or our intellectual ability, but rather to boast only in this: that we understand and know God, "the LORD, who exercises kindness, justice and righteousness on earth, for in these I delight" (9:23–24). Despite the fact that Jeremiah spoke these words more than twenty-five hundred years ago, he accurately identified the three things most admired in American society: money, looks, and brains. Our identity is not to be found in any of these. They will all prove to be false sources of meaning and self-worth.

This truth is so simple, yet we find it so hard to really make it a vital part of our daily living. Our calling is to be citizens in a kingdom that is worldwide and that involves all dimensions of human existence. That's the big picture and that is the frame of reference we need when we consider the question of jobs and careers.

A second and closely related truth is that our identity must be in our relationship to Jesus Christ, not in what we do or where we work. Here is another reason for avoiding the use of the word *calling* when we talk about our career aspirations. Misusing the word elevates the importance of work over other aspects of our lives, such as our role as members of a family or as members of a church community. It makes our employment sacred in a way that distorts our true understanding of our calling. Although God cares about every aspect of our lives, he is especially concerned about our personal relationship with him and the development of our character in the image of Christ; choices of where we live or how we earn a paycheck are much less significant to God.

A third biblical truth is this: as we consider the issue of our future in the marketplace, we need a "right estimate" of who we are. The apostle Paul instructs us, "Do not think of yourself more highly than you ought, but rather think of yourself with sober judgment" (Rom. 12:3). J. B. Phillips's translation states it this way: "Don't cherish exaggerated ideas of yourself or your importance, but try to have a sane estimate of your capabilities by the light of faith that God has given to you all."

We must not have inflated or deflated egos. Each extreme is harmful. This teaching, in the context of the apostle Paul's subsequent discussion of gifts in the family of faith, means that we need to be discerning about our own strengths and weaknesses. A sober estimate of our abilities is best achieved with the help of Christian friends who know us and with whom we are in close relationship. They are the ones who know our heart, who can help us assess where our talents are and what things excite our imaginations. The use of guidance and testing instruments which identify interests and abilities is another important way of achieving a "sane estimate" of ourselves.

A fourth biblical principle that is critical for us to recognize is this: when thinking about our jobs and careers, we must replace our focus on self with a focus on service. Many subtle and not-so-subtle influences of our culture emphasize self: self-fulfillment, self-satisfaction, self-actualization. What can *I* get out of my job? How can *I* be happy in my work? What do *I* enjoy doing the most?

In stark contrast to what our popular culture tells us, Scripture emphasizes the term *service*. Kingdom citizenship involves serving others. Remember the fundamental commandments of God: "Love the Lord your God with all your heart, and with all your soul, and with all your mind. . . . Love your neighbor as yourself"

(Matt. 22:37–39, RSV). Love God, yourself, and your neighbor. We cannot love ourselves or our neighbors if we do not love God, because he gives us the ability to love others. Nor will we love our neighbors if we do not love ourselves in the proper biblical sense. Love of others—as we love ourselves—is the radical new dimension that we need when we think about our own careers.

It is so easy for us to spiritualize biblical teaching on this subject and reduce it to vague abstract truths that somehow are important to our inner lives but not to the subject of our employment. Jesus said: "Whoever wants to become great among you must be your servant, and whoever wants to be first must be your slave—just as the Son of Man did not come to be served, but to serve . . ." (Matt. 20:26–28). Jesus described himself as "one who serves" (Luke 22:27, RSV). And he not only talked about serving others, but also did it! Jesus Christ, Lord of history, washed the feet of his disciples—an activity reserved for servants. When he finished washing their feet he said, "I have set you an example that you should do as I have done for you" (John 13:15).

If we took this teaching seriously our perspective on jobs and careers would be radically different from the prevailing view in our society. Work for Christians should never be viewed primarily as a means for material accumulation or for self-esteem, but rather as an opportunity to serve God and others. Instead of first asking "What can I get out of my job?" we ought to ask "In what area of service am I, as a minister of Christ, best able to bring reconciliation and wholeness to a broken world?" This is the biblical starting point for a correct view of work.

Scripture in effect changes the questions that we should be asking ourselves. If we first ask ourselves how we can serve others, it is implied that we have an accurate knowledge of our own abilities. But it also implies that we are able to assess the current and anticipated needs of the people of the world. That's why the emphasis on the big picture is so important. Meeting basic human needs, not wants, is our priority as Christians. Needs are those things which, if not met, keep a person from being able to live and respond to God's call.

A fifth biblical principle is this: all jobs are not of equal worth in God's sight. A biblical perspective on work suggests that work is a God-ordained activity and that labor is of value as we serve as stewards and co-creators in God's world. But cultural worth is another criterion of Christian teaching about work. If we are called to be servants, the work that we do must bring benefit to others—benefit that has significance. We should avoid not only jobs that are harmful by definition (gambling and prostitution, for example), but also work that results in no useful service. Using our abilities to develop, make, or sell people luxury items or articles that can be harmful is not a biblically sound choice of a career. That is not God's desire for us.

Once we ask ourselves what the needs are in our world and what our abilities are in light of those needs, the proper framework has been put in place. Simply to choose a career on the basis of our likes and dislikes will result in the selection of a job that has limited cultural worth. The biblical vision is one of men and women who, like Christ, are servants to a world that desperately needs the good news of salvation, a message of wholeness and healing and a message of God's grace which leads to eternal life.

So we are back to our original question: "Why work?" A summary of biblical teaching on work would be this: we work to serve God and bring glory to his name, to fulfill our distinctiveness as humans by being stewards and co-creators with God in the world, to provide for our needs and those of our families because that is what God intended, and to help others who are in need. Work, therefore, is service, not primarily for ourselves, but for God and for others.

A biblical understanding of work brings dignity to our labor when it is understood as service. It also sees work as involving social benefit. Work, rightfully understood, involves a contribution to the common good of society. It is not just "my own thing."

Scripture does not say much more than this on the subject of work. There are no how-to steps for busy North American evangelicals. The challenge we now face is to understand our situation in the light of these biblical truths. These truths are guidelines for us, but they do not answer all our detailed questions about exactly what job we should take or what a good starting salary is. That's what discipleship is all about: making choices in light of the biblical truths we have discerned.

We live in an exciting time. Jesus Christ has called us to be citizens of the kingdom of God, which is both a present reality and a future hope. We are members of the kingdom of God right now and can experience some of the benefits of that membership, but we will experience the kingdom in its fullest when Christ comes again in all his glory. In the meantime, we live in that critical epoch between Christ's advent and his second coming. We have been instructed to be kingdom agents in the world, to be salt and light. That's not only good evangelical theology; that's also good news because it gives us a purpose and a vision for our lives. It makes our lives meaningful. It gives us the answer to the question "Why work?"

Appendix 1:
Christian Professional and
Academic Associations

Athletics

Fellowship of Christian Athletes
8701 Leeds Road
Kansas City, MO 64129

Arts, Media, and Entertainment

Christian Theatre Artist Guild
P.O. Box 14157
Minneapolis, MN 55416

Christians in Visual Arts
P.O. Box 10247
Arlington, VA 22210

Fellowship of Christians in Arts, Media and Entertainment
P.O. Box 9323
Seattle, WA 98109

Business

Christian Business Men's Committee
1800 McCallie Avenue
Chattanooga, TN 37404

Downtown Disciples
% Probe Ministries
1900 Firman Drive
Suite 100
Richardson, TX 75081

Executive Christian Women
1523 Silver Strand Circle
Palatine, IL 60074

Fellowship of Companies for Christ
61 Perimeter Park, N.E.
Atlanta, GA 30341

Full Gospel Business Men's Fellowship
P.O. Box 5050
Costa Mesa, CA 92626

Intercristo
19303 Fremont Avenue
North Seattle, WA 98133

Economics

Association of Christian Economists
Professor John Mason
255 Grapevine Road
Wenham, MA 01984

Education

Christian Educators Association International
1410 W. Colorado Boulevard
Pasadena, CA 91105

History

Conference on Faith and History
Professor Richard Pierard, Secretary
Department of History
Indiana State University
Terre Haute, IN 47809

Law

Christian Legal Society
P.O. Box 1492
Merrifield, VA 22116

Lawyers Christian Fellowship
3931 E. Main Street
Columbus, OH 43213

Librarianship

Association of Christian Librarians
P.O. Box 4
Cedarville, OH 45314

Literature

The Conference on Christianity and Literature
Professor Roy Battenhouse, President

English Department
Indiana University
Bloomington, IN 47401

Mathematics
Association of Christian Mathematicians
Professor Robert Brabenec
Wheaton College
Wheaton, IL 60187

Medicine
Nurses Christian Fellowship
233 Langdon Street
Madison, WI 53703

Christian Medical Society
1616 Gateway Boulevard
P.O. Box 689
Richardson, TX 75080

Christian Dental Society
5235 Sky Trail
Littleton, CO 80123

Missionary Dentists
The Missionary Dentist Inc.
P.O. Box 7002
Seattle, WA 98133

Military Service
Christian Military Fellowship
Box 1207
Englewood, CO 80150

Officers' Christian Fellowship of the U.S.A.
Box 1177
Englewood, CO 80150

Music
Fellowship of Christian Musicians
P.O. Box 1092
Ponca City, OK 74602

Natural Sciences
American Scientific Affiliation
P.O. Box J
Ipswich, MA 01938

Philosophy
Society of Christian Philosophers
Professor Kenneth Konyndyk

Calvin College
Grand Rapids, MI 49506

Evangelical Philosophical Society
2011 Fallen Leaf Lane
Los Altos, CA 94022

Psychology

Christian Association for Psychological Studies
The University Hills Christian Center
26705 Farmington Road
Farmington Hills, MI 48018

Social Sciences and Humanities

Christians in the Social Sciences and Humanities
1429 N. Holyoke
Wichita, KS 67208

Social Work

National Association of Christians in Social Work
P.O. Box 90
St. Davids, PA 19087

Sociology

Christian Sociological Society
Dr. George A. Hillery, Jr.
Department of Sociology
V.P.I. and State University
Blacksburg, VA 24061

Appendix 2
Vocational Guidance Resources

Bolles, Richard N. *What Color Is Your Parachute? A Practical Manual for Job-Hunters and Career Changers.* 2d ed. Berkeley, Calif.: Ten Speed Press, 1984.

Casewit, Curtis W. *How to Get a Job Overseas.* 3d ed. New York: Arco, 1984.

Encyclopedia of Associations. 10th ed. Detroit: Gale Research, 1976.

Federal Research Service, Inc. *Federal Career Opportunities* (bi-weekly magazine). Vienna, Va.: FRS.

Gale, Barry, and Linda Gale. *Discover What You're Best At: The National Career Aptitude System and Career Directory.* New York: Simon and Schuster, 1982.

Kocher, Eric. *International Jobs: Where They Are, How to Get Them.* Menlo Park, Calif.: Addison-Wesley, 1984.

Pilder, Richard J., and William F. Pilder. *How to Find Your Life's Work: Staying Out of Traps and Taking Control of Your Career.* Englewood Cliffs, N.J.: Prentice-Hall, 1981.

Rockcastle, Madeline T., ed. *Where to Start: An Annotated Career-Planning Bibliography.* 4th ed. Princeton, N.J.: Peterson's Guides, 1983.

U.S. Department of Labor, Bureau of Labor Statistics. *Exploring Careers* (pamphlet series). Washington, D.C.: Government Printing Office, 1980.

————. *Occupational Outlook Handbook.* Washington, D.C.: Government Printing Office, 1986.

U.S. Department of Labor, Employment and Training Administration.

Dictionary of Occupational Titles. 4th ed. Washington, D.C.: Government Printing Office, 1977.

_____. *Guide for Occupational Exploration.* Washington, D.C.: Government Printing Office, 1979.

Selected Resources
for Further Study

In recent years the number of books by Christian authors dealing with the subject of careers and vocation has greatly increased. This expanded interest in the relationship of the Christian faith to the world of work is due in part to a growing evangelical awareness that Christ's lordship has implications for every aspect of one's life. The contribution of many of these recent books is uneven; some come close to merely baptizing predominant values in our culture with biblical language, while most focus almost exclusively on personal matters relating to one's careers with little emphasis on the larger issues of how a Christian view of work should affect our perspectives on labor unions, unemployment, or labor-management relations.

The following annotated list of resources focuses mainly on recent publications by Christian authors, publications in which at least some effort has been made to see the connecting points between our profession of faith in Jesus Christ and our view of work. The annotations generally emphasize the central focus and strengths of each resource.

Beckmann, David M., et al. *The Overseas List: Opportunities for Living and Working in Developing Countries.* Minneapolis: Augsburg, 1985.

This is a remarkable resource for people who would like to live and work in a developing country, spend just a year or two abroad, or do volunteer work abroad. It is a comprehensive review of nearly all the ways that United States citizens come to live or travel in developing countries and it is written especially for Christians who are looking for opportunities for service. This is an indispensable tool which has met a pressing need for Christians with a heart for service in the Two-Thirds World.

Catherwood, Fred. *On the Job: The Christian Nine to Five.* Grand Rapids: Zondervan, 1980.

The author provides an extremely thoughtful analysis of the relationship of faith to modern industrial society. Catherwood is a leading British industrialist and a member of the European Parliament. The author emphasizes service as the prime motivation in a Christian approach to work and includes an analysis of employment trends, the responsibilities of trade unions and management, and the role of central government in economic affairs.

Clark, Martin E. *Choosing Your Career: The Christian's Decision Manual.* Phillipsburg, N.J.: Presbyterian and Reformed, 1981.

This book includes chapters on biblical foundations for work, the nature of guidance, and the meaning of calling. The author argues against the separation of sacred and secular on the grounds that all Christians should view career choice as a response to the comprehensive call of God to salvation. It contains useful practical advice on self-evaluation and determining suitability for various careers.

Diehl, William E. *Christianity and Real Life.* Philadelphia: Fortress, 1976.

A central thesis of the book is that Protestant Christians have failed to practice the doctrine of the priesthood of all believers. Diehl, a manager of sales for the Bethlehem Steel Corporation, is particularly critical of the failure of local churches to relate their ministry to the world of work. In response to this failure, Diehl suggests strategies for how Christians can help one another relate their faith to the marketplace by means of house fellowship groups and mutual accountability. The book includes strategies for witnessing on the job both by word and ethical decision making.

Farnsworth, Kirk E., and Wendell H. Lawhead. *Life Planning: A Christian Approach to Careers.* Downers Grove: InterVarsity, 1981.

The goal of this workbook is to help readers develop a lifetime approach to evaluating their jobs and themselves. Through a series of twelve sessions designed for small-group use, the book facilitates the discovery of one's values, abilities, gifts, and interests; it also provides helpful advice on making decisions and investigating career opportunities.

Frey, Bradshaw, et al. *At Work and Play.* Jordan Station, Ontario: Paideia, 1986.

Four representatives of the Coalition for Christian Outreach relate faith to various academic disciplines, vocation, and leisure. The book is aimed at the Christian student at a secular college or university and the following academic disciplines are covered: education, sociology, the sciences, and psychology. The authors emphasize the responsibility that Christian students have to master material from the secular world view while learning to critique that world view in the light of Christian perspectives.

Gibbs, Mark. *Christians with Secular Power.* Philadelphia: Fortress, 1981.

This is a book aimed at stimulating Christian laypersons in the exercise of their ministry, particularly in the secular world. After giving a brief introduction which emphasizes the responsibility of the laity to fully understand their common calling, the author focuses on special occupations where power is constantly wielded. It is here—in politics, business, labor unions, law enforcement, military service, and the media—where Christians must constantly be aware of their opportunities to minister.

Hardy, Lee. "The Christian and Career Choice." Grand Rapids: CRC Publications, 1985.

The pamphlet offers a concise and cogent analysis of the subject. Hardy compares Reformed approaches to vocation with Greek and medieval Christian thinking. The primary sense of vocation for Hardy is the call of the gospel of salvation. The pamphlet emphasizes the importance of identifying and matching God-given talents with the areas of social need. Hardy discusses the danger of workaholism and attacks the myth of "one right job" for every individual.

Heiges, Donald R. *The Christian's Calling.* Philadelphia: Fortress, 1984.

The author begins with a description of the plight of men and women who lack a sense of vocation in the midst of a computer age and the robotization of industry. He then concentrates on the biblical view of vocation—the Christian's calling—and on Martin Luther's insights on that subject. This helpful study, originally published in 1958 and reissued in 1984, concludes with a chapter on "Vocation as Ministry."

Henry, Carl F. H. *Aspects of Christian Social Ethics.* 1964. Grand Rapids: Baker, 1980.

Chapter 2 is one of the most thoughtful Protestant approaches to the topic of work. Henry sees work as a daily-traveled bridge between theology and social ethics and therefore of vital importance for all Christians. The meaning of calling in the New Testament is discussed together with the historical development of the theology of work. Henry reflects upon technological displacement, worker/management relations, and criteria for selecting a career.

Hybels, Bill. *Christians in the Marketplace.* Wheaton: Victor Books, 1982.

Hybels writes in a lively, conversational manner and provides numerous examples from daily life. He relates Scripture to such practical issues as dealing with anger and difficult relationships in the workplace, time management, the stewardship of personal finances, and decision making. Hybels also provides a forceful exposure of the deceitful aspects of advertising and the role of the devil in the development of wrong attitudes toward work. The book comes with a study and teachers' guide for a thirteen-session adult education elective.

John Paul II. *On Human Work.* Washington, D.C.: Catholic Conference, 1981.

This encyclical represents the shift in the Roman Catholic understanding of vocation and the latest stage in the breakdown of the traditional division between the sacred and the secular. The theological analysis emphasizes the subjective dimension of labor, with work being created for man and not man for work. This person-centered approach provides the basis for ethical directives in the context of human rights. Issues dealt with include the role of unions, the primacy of family, employment policy, and disabled workers.

Larramore, Darryl. *Careers: A Guide for Parents and Counselors.* Provo, Utah: Brigham Young University Press, 1978.

Although somewhat outdated, this manual is designed to help parents and professional counselors advise young people about their future careers. In addition to practical activities that help readers determine their own interests, aptitudes, and values, this book offers practical counsel about expanding our awareness of career opportunities and beginning the process of a job search. The central theme is this: choose a lifestyle and plan an education adapted to a variety of jobs.

Marshall, Paul, et al. *Labour of Love: Essays on Work.* Toronto: Wedge, 1980.

This is a well-written and thought-provoking work. The authors, who include academics and representatives of the Christian Labour Association of Canada, accuse evangelicals of failing to grasp the normative character of God's revelation for social, economic, and political life. Their desire is to place matters pertaining to personal career within the wider context of economic and political life. They provide a fine theological and historical survey of the purpose and nature of work before reflecting upon the future of labor in the areas of employment policy, technology, and industrial relations.

Mattson, Ralph, and Arthur Miller. *Finding a Job You Can Love.* Nashville: Thomas Nelson, 1982.

This book provides vocational guidance principles based upon the System for Identifying Motivated Abilities (SIMA). The authors claim that three or four out of five workers are in the wrong job, largely because they have not correctly identified their God-given gifts and motivations. Vocational choice is discussed in relation to spiritual maturity. There is a useful description of some worldly traps, including too great a concern for salary and constant job-hopping. An appendix contains the SIMA method of aiding career selection.

Moran, Pamela J. *The Christian Job Hunter: A Step-by-Step Guide to Career Planning.* Ann Arbor: Servant, 1984.

The author provides practical step-by-step advice to help you define your career goals, identify your skills, and learn how to interview with a prospective employer. The theme is that each of us should engage in an informed, purposeful search for a job that puts our God-given skills and ability to best use.

Pountney, Michael. *Getting a Job: A Guide for Choosing a Career.* Downers Grove: InterVarsity, 1984.

Pountney provides interesting variation by basing his book upon the experiences of eight University of British Columbia students over a two-year period as they decide on and implement career plans. The students discuss particular problems of the baby-boom career market: restricted vocational opportunities, the pressures of climbing the ladder, and the search for gratifying work in the context of large corporations. This is a valuable consideration of nontraditional career options focusing upon service to marginal members of society.

Rush, Myron. *Lord of the Marketplace.* Wheaton: Victor Books, 1986.

The author offers practical suggestions for how Christians should understand the marketplace as a mission field, how Christians should handle stress, and how Christian values can be preserved in a competitive corporate environment. Biblical principles are also discussed as they relate to business ethics and to success in running a business.

Shelly, Judith Allen. *Not Just a Job: Serving Christ in Your Work.* Downers Grove: InterVarsity, 1985.

This is one of the best of the popular treatments of the subject, written in a colloquial style with numerous personal illustrations.

Shelly, a seminary graduate and former Nurses' Christian Fellowship staff worker, views work as a primary expression of our faith and praise to God. It involves service to others and the stewardship of our gifts and represents the most effective means of communicating the gospel to the world. The author provides advice on dealing with pressure, time management, money, and status. She stresses the importance of Christian fellowship as a source of guidance for vocational choice. This book gives a rare treatment of the issues arising from two-career families, marriage, and singleness, and a provocative discussion of women in Scripture as they relate to work.

Vos, Nelvin. *Seven Days a Week: Faith in Action*. Philadelphia: Fortress, 1985.

This book focuses on how the experiences and feelings of daily life intersect with our Christian faith. Beginning with a discussion of how all of God's people are called to ministry (he calls the people of God "priests with a vocation"), the author then analyzes the various arenas in which the laity are already settled in ministry, such as family, occupation, work, leisure, community, and church.

Index of Scripture References

Member Institutions of the Christian College Coalition

Anderson College
Anderson, IN 46012

Asbury College
Wilmore, KY 40390

Azusa Pacific University
Azusa, CA 91702

Bartlesville Wesleyan
College
Bartlesville, OK 74003

Belhaven College
Jackson, MS 39202

Bethany Nazarene
College
Bethany, OK 73008

Bethel College
Mishawaka, IN 46545

Bethel College
North Newton, KS
67117

Bethel College
3900 Bethel Drive
St. Paul, MN 55112

Biola University
13800 Biola Avenue
La Mirada, CA 90639

Bryan College
Dayton, TN 37321

Calvin College
Grand Rapids, MI
49506

Campbell University
Buies Creek, NC 27506

Campbellsville College
Campbellsville, KY
42718

Central Wesleyan
College
Central, SC 29630

Colorado Christian
College
Lakewood, CO 80226

Covenant College
Lookout Mountain, TN
37350

Dallas Baptist
Dallas, TX 75211

Dordt College
Sioux Center, IA 51250

Eastern College
St. Davids, PA 19087

Eastern Mennonite
College
Harrisonburg, VA 22801

Eastern Nazarene
College
23 E. Elm Avenue
Quincy, MA 02170

Evangel College
Springfield, MO 65802

Fresno Pacific College
Fresno, CA 93702

Geneva College
Beaver Falls, PA 15010

George Fox College
Newberg, OR 97132

Gordon College
Wenham, MA 01984

Goshen College
Goshen, IN 46526

Grace College
200 Seminary Drive
Winona Lake, IN 46590

Grand Canyon College
P.O. Box 11097
Phoenix, AZ 85061

Greenville College
Greenville, IL 62246

Houghton College
Houghton, NY 14744

Huntington College
Huntington, IN 46750

John Brown University
Siloam Springs, AR
72761

Judson College
Elgin, IL 60120

King College
Bristol, TN 37620

The King's College
Briarcliff Manor, NY
10510

Lee College
Cleveland, TN 37311

LeTourneau College
Longview, TX 75607

Malone College
Canton, OH 44709

Marion College
Marion, IN 46952

The Master's College
Newhall, CA 91322

Messiah College
Grantham, PA 17027

Mid-America Nazarene
College
Olathe, KS 66061

Milligan College
Milligan College, TN
37682

Mississippi College
Clinton, MS 39058

Mount Vernon
Nazarene College
Mt. Vernon, OH 43050

North Park College
5125 North Spaulding
Ave.
Chicago, IL 60625

Northwest Christian
College
11th and Alder
Eugene, OR 97401

Northwest Nazarene
College
Nampa, ID 83651

Northwestern College
Orange City, IA 51041

Northwestern College
3003 Snelling N.
Roseville, MN 55113

Nyack College
Nyack, NY 10960

Olivet Nazarene College
Kankakee, IL 60901

Oral Roberts University
7777 South Lewis
Tulsa, OK 74171

Palm Beach Atlantic
College
1101 South Olive
Avenue
West Palm Beach, FL
33401

Point Loma Nazarene
College
3900 Lomaland Drive
San Diego, CA 92106

Roberts Wesleyan
College
2301 Westside Drive
Rochester, NY 14624

Seattle Pacific
University
Seattle, WA 98119

Simpson College
San Francisco, CA
94134

Sioux Falls College
Sioux Falls, SD 57101

Southern California
College
55 Fair Drive
Costa Mesa, CA 92626

Spring Arbor College
Spring Arbor, MI 49283

Sterling College
Sterling, KS 67579

Tabor College
Hillsboro, KS 67063

Taylor University
Upland, IN 46989

Trevecca Nazarene
College
333 Murfreesboro Road
Nashville, TN 37210

Trinity College
2077 Half Day Road
Deerfield, IL 60015

Trinity Christian College
6601 West College Drive
Palos Heights, IL 60463

Warner Pacific College
2219 Southeast 68th
Avenue
Portland, OR 97215

Warner Southern
College
Lake Wales, FL 33853

Westmont College
955 La Paz Road
Santa Barbara, CA
93108

Wheaton College
Wheaton, IL 60187

Whitworth College
Spokane, WA 99251